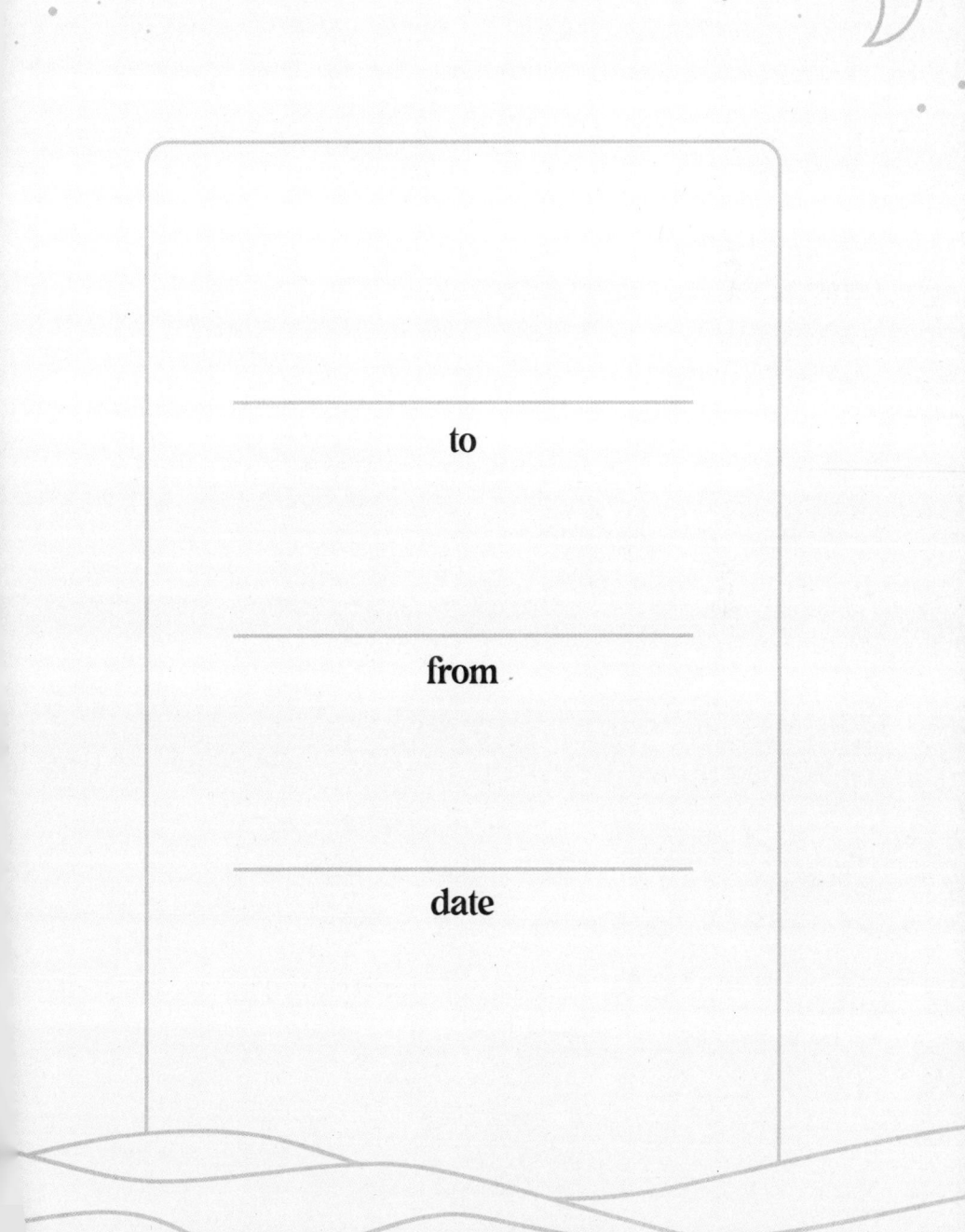

to

from

date

sleep psalms

NIGHTLY MOMENTS
of MINDFULNESS *and* REST

PRAY.COM

Published by:

21154 Highway 16 East
Siloam Springs, AR 72761
dayspring.com

Written by: Pray.com
Additional content collaboration provided by: Lisa Stilwell
Cover Design by: Greg Jackson of thinkpen.design

Printed in China
Prime: U1296
ISBN: 979-888-602-4357

Note to the Reader

You've likely picked up this book because you have trouble sleeping peacefully, that true soul rest that we all long for. *Sleep Psalms: Nightly Moments of Mindfulness and Rest* was created to remind you of the truth of God's Word and the promises of God that will reassure your heart and mind as you wind down from the day. Many of the psalms you'll read were written by David, a man of great faith who struggled with doubt, insecurity, temptation, and sin. Even in his darkest moments, David turned to God, crying out to Him, and was met with the voice of a loving, kind, and forgiving God. We have been gifted the Psalms, which provide insight into God's heart for you and remind you that you can give your worries and your troubles over to Him each day, knowing He can handle them.

As you read through the first 100 psalms, you'll enjoy short reflections, excerpts from God's Word, and a method of prayer called ACTS (adoration, confession, thanksgiving, and supplication).

- Adoration means to thank and praise God for who He is. Under the adoration section, you will pray through an attribute, or characteristic, of God.

- Confession means to look internally and admit your sins to the Lord. You do this so that you can unburden your heart and receive His loving forgiveness. Confession is difficult, but it is met with a forgiveness that allows you to relax into the kindness of the Lord.

- Thanksgiving means to offer words of thanks to God for all that He has blessed you with. This realigns your heart, even on your worst days, reminding you of all the good gifts He has placed in your life.

- Supplication is another word for prayer. In this section, you will close each night with a prayer to the Lord that will calm your heart and prepare you for a night of rest.

Whether you've been following God for a while or are just starting your journey, *Sleep Psalms* will help you to align yourself with the promises of God for rest and restoration and prepare you for a good night's sleep.

Table of Contents

Table of Contents

Psalm 1

Tonight, or any night, we can find peace in knowing God's words of truth can and will sustain us. When we take delight in them, we will be blessed and refreshed. Take a moment now to clear your mind of the day and focus your thoughts on God by remembering who He is—the all-powerful One who knows you, sees you, and dearly loves you. He knows the weight of the burdens you are carrying, and He is ready to lift them and give you rest for your mind, body, and soul.

Bring today's worries and anxieties to Him and know that He cares for you and each challenge you face. Focus on His promises for you and His goodness. Keep your mind and heart still and silent to hear His voice. Ask for Him to speak to you through His Word. Believe and do not doubt that His voice will lead you to a safe, quiet place where you can surrender to Him.

> Blessed is the one
>> who does not walk in step with the wicked
> or stand in the way that sinners take
>> or sit in the company of mockers,
> but whose delight is in the law of the LORD,
>> and who meditates on His law day and night.
> That person is like a tree planted by streams of water,
>> which yields its fruit in season
> and whose leaf does not wither—
>> whatever they do prospers.
> Not so the wicked!
>> They are like chaff
> that the wind blows away.
> Therefore the wicked will not stand in the judgment,
>> nor sinners in the assembly of the righteous.
> For the LORD watches over the way of the righteous,
>> but the way of the wicked leads to destruction.

PSALM 1

ADORATION: Let yourself bask in God's presence; feel His peace wash over you. Imagine being firmly rooted in His love, grace, and truth and quenching your thirst in His springs of eternal life. Know God can sustain you where you are. Praise Him for always keeping His promises and for being your firm foundation.

CONFESSION: Reflect on your life and think of areas He has asked you to surrender to Him. Have you allowed anything or anyone to distract you from His way?

Breathe in God's forgiveness. As you exhale, let go of any guilt or shame. Receive the love He has for you, and find inner peace and rest for your mind, body, and soul.

THANKSGIVING: Praise God from whom all blessings flow—blessings of protection, grace, forgiveness, and the people He's brought onto your path and given opportunities to pray for and to minister His love.

SUPPLICATION: *Father, I thank You for Your promise to watch over me tonight. Help me to surrender all the cares of this day to You so that I can be still and rest in Your care. I take delight in Your Word and meditate on it now so that my faith will grow, and I am able to trust in You for all things.*

Psalm 2

Even though life can feel out of control sometimes, you can find rest in knowing God is in complete control over every detail of your life. No matter what's going on, you can find peace in His power and hope in knowing that when you place your trust in Him, you will be blessed.

As you prepare to receive His Word for today, take a few moments to relax your body, clear your mind, and settle your heart. Close your eyes and breathe in and out slowly to release the stress in your muscles. Feel your joints soften and your feet relax. Take another deep breath and clear your mind.

Focus your thoughts on the goodness of God. Lift up your worship and praise as you remember who He is—the Almighty One who works every day and night on your behalf. He is working now to relieve you of your stress from today and to give you peaceful rest through the night. Surrender to Him and listen to His voice of truth from the following passage of Scripture:

> Why do the nations conspire
>   and the peoples plot in vain? . . .
> The One enthroned in heaven laughs;
>   the Lord scoffs at them.
> He rebukes them in His anger
>   and terrifies them in His wrath, saying,
> "I have installed My king
>   on Zion, My holy mountain."
> I will proclaim the LORD's decree:
> He said to Me, "You are My Son;
>   today I have become your Father.
> Ask Me,
>   and I will make the nations Your inheritance,
>   the ends of the earth Your possession. . . ."
> Therefore, you kings, be wise;
>   be warned, you rulers of the earth.
> Serve the Lord with fear

and celebrate His rule with trembling. . . .
Blessed are all who take refuge in Him.

PSALM 2:1, 4–8, 10–12

ADORATION: When this world becomes too much to bear, take refuge in God, knowing He reigns over all the nations and the rulers, over every aspect of our lives. Nothing happens without His knowing and approval. Nothing falls from His grasp. Nothing surprises Him. He responds to everything that happens in this world, and He knows what to do in every situation.

CONFESSION: Think of a time when circumstances made you fearful and hindered your relationship with God. Give those fears to Him, and He will put them to rest tonight.

THANKSGIVING: Praise Him for taking your fears and helping you find rest. Praise Him for how He blesses your life. Praise Him for all the good things He is doing.

SUPPLICATION: *Father, thank You that I can cast all my cares on You. Please fill me with Your peace and surround me with comfort that helps my heart and mind to release the worries of this day into Your hands. Be with me as I put my trust in You and rest in knowing that You are indeed in control of all things. Amen.*

Psalm 3

Have you considered that you can find rest and have confidence in the midst of troubled times? Well you can, because God is your shield—He protects you, and He loves you. He can and will deliver you from your trials, no matter how great or small. Just put your trust and faith in Him; claim with boldness the truths in His promises for you.

As you clear your mind and focus your thoughts on God, remember who He is—the all-powerful One who knows you, sees you, loves you, and sustains you. Focus on believing He is for you.

As you prepare to meditate on God's Word, take in a deep breath and exhale any stress and tension in your muscles. As you relax your body, open your mind and heart to hear God's voice. Ask Him to speak to you, then listen for His still, small voice to lead you down a safe, secure path. Soak in these powerful words written just for you:

> LORD, how many are my foes!
>   How many rise up against me!
> Many are saying of me,
>   "God will not deliver him."
> But You, LORD, are a shield around me,
>   my glory, the One who lifts my head high.
> I call out to the LORD,
>   and He answers me from His holy mountain.
> I lie down and sleep;
>   I wake again, because the LORD sustains me.
> I will not fear though tens of thousands
>   assail me on every side. . . .
> From the LORD comes deliverance.
>   May Your blessing be on Your people.
>
>   PSALM 3:1-6, 8

ADORATION: Take a moment to focus on God's unlimited power and strength to protect you, sustain you, and defend you. Know there is no battle or obstacle too big for God to overcome. Allow the Lord to sustain you with His power and strength as you lie down to sleep. Praise Him for His faithfulness to see you through your hardships in life.

CONFESSION: Think about times when you allowed worry and anxiety to keep you up at night rather than putting your trust in God. Have you tried to overcome your troubles on your own? Be filled with His forgiveness and let go of your guilt and shame. Surrender to God's love and find inner peace and rest.

THANKSGIVING: Praise Him for the times He has delivered you from your troubles. Praise Him for the peace and calm He gave you during a crisis. Praise Him for the ways He has protected you throughout your life. Praise Him for how He will continue to deliver you without end.

SUPPLICATION: *Lord, I come to You now and lay my heart before You. Rise up and deliver me from the troubles I face right now. I pray for Your protection and the peace it gives to sustain me through this night as I sleep on into tomorrow—a whole new day to walk in Your presence. Amen.*

Psalm 4

The best way to prepare your heart to hear and receive God's promises for you is to be still. So, as you turn off the concerns of the day, close your eyes and calm your mind. Take a deep breath and allow all the negatives and stressors to flow right out of your body. Now open your eyes and invite God's presence into your heart and fill it with His truth. Be still and know that God is with you, ready to renew your mind and spirit.

You can find great comfort in knowing God hears your prayers and He will give you relief from your worries and fears. King David knew this all too well as he wrote this night prayer that has comforted so many over the centuries:

> *Answer me when I call to You,*
>   *my righteous God.*
> *Give me relief from my distress;*
>   *have mercy on me and hear my prayer.*
> *How long will you people turn my glory into shame?*
>   *How long will you love delusions and seek false gods?*
> *Know that the* LORD *has set apart His faithful servant for Himself;*
>   *the Lord hears when I call to Him.*
> *Tremble and do not sin;*
>   *when you are on your beds,*
>   *search your hearts and be silent.*
> *Offer the sacrifices of the righteous*
>   *and trust in the* LORD.
> *Many,* LORD, *are asking, "Who will bring us prosperity?"*
>   *Let the light of Your face shine on us.*
> *Fill my heart with joy*
>   *when their grain and new wine abound.*
> *In peace I will lie down and sleep,*
>   *for You alone,* LORD,
>   *make me dwell in safety.*

PSALM 4

ADORATION: The Bible tells us to turn to God in our distress and lay our requests before Him. Let's find comfort in knowing God is with us and He hears our cry. Nothing and no one can overcome the power and the strength of the Lord. You are safe. You are secure. You are loved. Take delight in His favor and feel the gladness He has put in your heart.

CONFESSION: Be still and quiet before God. Search your heart. Ask Him to reveal any sin in your life and ask for His forgiveness—*then receive it*. Remember that God can use all the brokenness in your life, including your mistakes and failures. He will redeem whatever is lost; His mercies are great and new every morning.

THANKSGIVING: Thank the Lord for His gracious forgiveness. Praise Him for choosing you and setting you apart to do His good work. Think of a specific time you have called out to God, and He responded. Thank Him for hearing your prayers and for answering as only He can.

SUPPLICATION: *Father, help my heart to be still and reflect on the gift of Your presence in my life. I trust in You and am committed to following Your ways. Help me to find Your joy no matter how I am serving You. Guide me in Your truth as I strive to bring You glory. Help me to rest securely in Your love as I lay me down to sleep. All praise to You. Amen.*

Psalm 5

In today's fast-paced world, it's hard to find a place to escape from getting caught up in such a whirlwind. Fear and demands and pressures can mount so high, where can you go to find peace and rest? As you breathe in for air and exhale your day, close your eyes and take refuge in God. He is your shelter of love and peace for your soul that no one or thing can provide. Reflect on the times God has been faithful to you and be confident He will continue to be faithful. Bring all your troubles and worries to Him. Inhale and exhale slowly and allow His joy and hope to fill your heart and His peace to fill your mind.

Tonight, lay your requests before the Lord and wait expectantly, trusting He will hear you and pour out His blessings and favor upon you. As you wait on the Lord to answer, find solace in His Word.

> Listen to my words, LORD,
>   consider my lament.
> Hear my cry for help,
>   my King and my God,
>   for to You I pray.
> In the morning, LORD, You hear my voice;
>   in the morning I lay my requests before You
>   and wait expectantly. . . .
> By Your great love,
>   [I] can come into Your house;
> in reverence I bow down
>   toward Your holy temple.
> Lead me, LORD, in Your righteousness
>   because of my enemies—
>   make Your way straight before me. . . .
> Let all who take refuge in You be glad;
>   let them ever sing for joy.
> Spread Your protection over them,
>   that those who love Your name may rejoice in You.
> Surely, LORD, You bless the righteous;
>   You surround them with Your favor as with a shield.

PSALM 5:1–3, 7–8, 11–12

ADORATION: The Bible tells us our God is the God of truth. Nothing can stand against Him or His Word. He reveals the lies of our enemies and defends us from the lies spoken against us. His light will expose the darkness around us. His truth and justice will prevail. And His love will sustain us through the darkest of nights. Rejoice and be glad in Him!

CONFESSION: Have any lies come out of your mouth recently? Have you ever rebelled against the Lord and followed your own path? If so, maybe it's time to ask God to forgive you. Then let God's grace and mercy wash over you. Trust and know that your sins are forgiven.

THANKSGIVING: Thank the Lord for leading you on His path of life. Thank Him for protecting you and keeping you from evil. Think of all the ways He has been a refuge where you know you are safe and filled with His favor.

SUPPLICATION: *Father, I look to You to make my way straight and to lead me into righteousness. I take shelter in Your arms and rest in the protection You provide in a world that is often hard to live in. I place my home and family in the shelter of Your arms of safety and thank You for the comfort this brings. In Jesus' name. Amen.*

Psalm 6

No matter what kinds of trials we face and struggles life brings our way, the Bible tells us we can find rest in God, knowing He is merciful and ready to forgive. He understands our struggles and is only a prayer away.

As you lie down tonight, close your eyes and breathe in and out slowly. Clear your mind by focusing your thoughts on God. Remember who He is—your Savior who loves you, pursues you, and rescues you. He knows the weight of what you are carrying from today, and He is ready to lift your burdens.

God's Word makes it clear: Nothing can separate us from Him—not our sin, not the brokenness in our world, not the troubles the enemy brings upon us. Know God is always here to rescue, to help, and to heal. As you read today's Scripture, make these words your own; know that He hears you and accepts your prayer.

> *Have mercy on me, LORD, for I am faint;*
> *heal me, Lord, for my bones are in agony.*
> *My soul is in deep anguish.*
> *How long, LORD, how long?*
> *Turn, LORD, and deliver me;*
> *save me because of Your unfailing love. . . .*
> *I am worn out from my groaning.*
> *All night long I flood my bed with weeping*
> *and drench my couch with tears.*
> *My eyes grow weak with sorrow;*
> *they fail because of all my foes.*
> *Away from me, all you who do evil,*
> *for the LORD has heard my weeping.*
> *The LORD has heard my cry for mercy;*
> *the LORD accepts my prayer.*

> **PSALM 6:2-4, 6-9**

ADORATION: Allow yourself to find comfort in His Word, which brings nourishment to your bones and peace to anxious hearts. Turn to the Lord and bask in His presence. Allow His mercy and love to wash over you. Know His mercy and grace are sufficient for you—His power is made perfect in your weakness. You have nothing to fear. Take a moment to worship God for His unfailing love and compassion and feel the peace He gives for your mind and your soul.

CONFESSION: Reflect on your circumstances to see what is troubling you today. If there is something you have said or done that led to your troubles, ask for God's forgiveness and mercy. He is here to forgive you and redeem you, not to punish you or forsake you. Confess any shame you are holding on to and allow God to fill you with hope and love.

THANKSGIVING: Think about the times God has shown you kindness and compassion. Thank Him for His mercy and grace. Thank Him for the times He has healed you or delivered you from troubling circumstances. Praise Him for His faithfulness to redeem and restore your life.

SUPPLICATION: *Lord, I cast all my cares on You right now and look to You for help through the troubles of my heart. Have mercy on me and help me to walk in Your grace. Bless my heart and mind with Your peace for sound rest through this night. Refresh my soul and lead me in a way that keeps me close to You in all that I do. In Your sweet name, I pray. Amen.*

Psalm 7

When we encounter injustice, it's comforting to know we can take refuge in God and find rest in knowing His justice will prevail—in our lives and in our world. That's why it's important to take time every day to remember who God is and to acknowledge His power.

Close your eyes, quiet your mind, and focus your thoughts on God. He is your shield that covers and protects you through the night. He is also your Savior who knows the pain and suffering you see all around as well as the details of what you're facing now. He knows the burdens you are carrying from today, and He wants to give you rest. Take comfort in the following verses and claim them as your own.

LORD my God, I seek refuge in You;
save me from all my pursuers and rescue me. . . .
Let the evil of the wicked come to an end,
but establish the righteous.
The one who examines the thoughts and emotions
is a righteous God.
My shield is with God,
who saves the upright in heart.
God is a righteous judge
and a God who shows His wrath every day. . . .
I will thank the LORD for His righteousness;
I will sing about the name of the LORD Most High.

PSALM 7:1, 9–11, 17 CSB

ADORATION: God warns us there will be injustice in this world. There may even be times when the wicked prosper and the righteous suffer. In these moments, it's vital to remember that God is always with us; He is our shield that protects us; His righteousness rescues us from despair. Take comfort knowing God makes us secure in His grace and love. And He will help you dwell in safety tonight.

Imagine God ruling from His magnificent throne in heaven. Feel the warmth of His light on your face. See His mighty hands, shielding you, holding you, keeping you safe through whatever storm you are in.

CONFESSION: God knows you better than anyone, even better than you know yourself. He knows what is in your heart and on your mind. Nothing can be hidden from Him. Ask God to forgive any unconfessed sin you may have in your life. Ask Him to forgive you for times you have hurt others unintentionally. Take comfort in knowing you are fully known and fully loved by your heavenly Father.

THANKSGIVING: God is a God of truth. Praise Him for the things He has made right in the past and for the things He has yet to make right in your life.

SUPPLICATION: *Father, help me to remember and rest in knowing that You see all things, and that Your justice will prevail in due time. Show me how to take a stand on behalf of the vulnerable and the oppressed, then give me the courage to do it. Give me the patience I need to wait on You and trust that You are in control. Help me to have Your perfect peace as I release the day and my concerns to You. Amen.*

Psalm 8

Tonight, as you lie down, you can rest assured that you are seen, you are important, and you are more than enough. You are incredibly valuable to the Almighty God! Relax, close your eyes, and breathe in God and breathe out any negative thoughts about yourself.

Remember that the Creator of the universe, who spoke the world into existence, also created you—His beautiful child, whom He perfectly crafted and whom He dearly loves and values. You are crowned with glory and honor!

> LORD, our Lord,
>   how majestic is Your name in all the earth!
> You have set Your glory in the heavens. . . .
> When I consider Your heavens,
>   the work of Your fingers,
> the moon and the stars,
>   which You have set in place,
> what is mankind that You are mindful of them,
>   human beings that You care for them?
> You have made them a little lower than the angels
>   and crowned them with glory and honor.
> You made them rulers over the works of Your hands;
>   You put everything under their feet. . . .
> LORD, our Lord,
>   how majestic is Your name in all the earth!

PSALM 8:1, 3-6, 9

ADORATION: Close your eyes and imagine God looking down on you in love. Know God made you and values you over all creation. You are His masterpiece. He has put His creation underneath your feet and has put you over the wonderful works of His hands because He loves you and adores you. Now adore Him in return for all that He has done. Take delight in the Lord; rejoice in His excellent name.

CONFESSION: Think of an area of your life in which you struggle with fully embracing the value you have in God's eyes. Bring your feelings of inadequacy to Him. Listen for His voice and let His tender whispers remind you of who you are in Him—His beloved child, who is more than enough, who is greatly loved, and who was created to do amazing things through Him.

THANKSGIVING: Thank God for the unique way He created you. Thank Him for the gifts He has given you in your life. Thank Him for His magnificence and for caring for and nurturing you, His beautiful creation.

SUPPLICATION: *Father, thank You for reminding me that my confidence comes from who I am in You—I am fearfully and wonderfully made. May I be reminded and may I believe that I am worthy of Your love and able to be used by You. Give me childlike faith as I sleep tonight so I can rest deeply in Your loving arms. All praise be to You. Amen.*

Psalm 9

Tonight, we can find hope and joy in God's Word. His Word reminds us that we can trust Him completely, for He sees us and hears us, and He will never forsake us. We can take delight in what the Lord has done and be assured of what He will do on our behalf in the future.

As you lie down, clear your mind and focus your thoughts on God; remember who He is—the all-powerful One who knows you, sees you, loves you, and sustains you. He knows every detail that troubles your heart, and He is ready to show His presence and give you rest for your mind, body, and soul. Close your eyes and listen for His voice of truth. Rest in His peace, knowing full well that He is for you.

> I will give thanks to You, LORD, with all my heart;
>   I will tell of all Your wonderful deeds....
> For You have upheld my right and my cause,
>   sitting enthroned as the righteous judge....
> The LORD reigns forever;
>   He has established His throne for judgment.
> He rules the world in righteousness
>   and judges the peoples with equity.
> The LORD is a refuge for the oppressed,
>   a stronghold in times of trouble.
> Those who know your name trust in You,
>   for You, LORD, have never forsaken those who seek You.
> Sing the praises of the LORD, enthroned in Zion;
>   proclaim among the nations what He has done.
> For He who avenges blood remembers;
>   He does not ignore the cries of the afflicted.

PSALM 9:1, 4, 7–12

ADORATION: Think about the goodness of a perfectly just, righteous God. He hears the cry of the afflicted and listens, ruling the world in righteousness. He judges with equity. He upholds your just cause with His right hand. He will never forget the needy. He will never turn His back on you.

CONFESSION: Think of a difficult circumstance you are holding on to instead of relinquishing to God. Is it time to talk to Him about your struggles with trusting Him? Have you ever taken matters into your own hands? Ask for His forgiveness and for His help with trusting Him completely.

THANKSGIVING: Praise God for His justice. Praise God for the hope He has given you during the dark times and for the hope He has given you for your future. Praise Him for the times He has provided for you. Thank Him for answering your prayers.

SUPPLICATION: *Lord, I cast all my cares and anxieties on You this night. I ask You to help me trust that Your ways are better than my ways; You are wise and know the bigger picture than I have in view. Give me eyes to see the needs of those around me and show me how to love and serve them the way Jesus did. I wait expectantly on You. In Jesus' name. Amen.*

Psalm 10

God is always listening with love to you and your prayers, even when you are unsure of whether He will hear and respond to you. He sees you and wants to bring you hope and peace as you turn to Him. You can find hope for your future and tranquility in your present by focusing on God's strength and power.

As you lie down and close your eyes, breathe in and out slowly, and focus your thoughts on God. Visualize Him as the powerful and righteous King, who sees all things. Embrace the truth that He is not only in complete control of every nation but also the circumstances you are in. Draw close to Him, and He will draw close to you. Listen for His still, small voice that brings comfort as only He can. Meditate on these consoling words to reassure your heart and bring you peaceful rest for the night.

> Why, Lord, do You stand far off?
>> Why do You hide Yourself in times of trouble? . . .
> Arise, Lord! Lift up Your hand, O God.
>> Do not forget the helpless. . . .
> You, God, see the trouble of the afflicted;
>> You consider their grief and take it in hand.
> The victims commit themselves to You;
>> You are the helper of the fatherless. . . .
> The Lord is King for ever and ever;
>> the nations will perish from His land.
> You, Lord, hear the desire of the afflicted;
>> You encourage them, and You listen to their cry,
> defending the fatherless and the oppressed,
>> so that mere earthly mortals
>> will never again strike terror.

PSALM 10:1, 12, 14, 16–18

ADORATION: Looking to the Almighty God can shift your perspective and transform your entire outlook. Remember that He is good, and He will never leave you—nothing can separate Him from you. Bask in His healing presence now and feel the warmth and closeness of His love.

CONFESSION: Think of any doubts you have about the goodness of God. Have you shared these doubts with Him? Maybe it's time for you to ask for forgiveness for not putting your trust in Him. Allow tonight's psalm to remind you of His supreme virtue and to renew your spirit of belief.

THANKSGIVING: Praise God for being with you when you face troubles. Rejoice in never having to face them or this world alone. Praise Him for the times He has helped you and delivered you in your past and how He will do the same in your future.

SUPPLICATION: *Lord, it's hard not to get overwhelmed. I ask that Your hand be on me as well as on all who are weak and vulnerable, that we would know of Your love and presence in our lives. Give me discernment and wisdom to not get pulled in all directions, but to stay safe within the path and plan You have for me. Help me to remember that You see the trouble of the afflicted and that You are in control. Help me to hold on to the truth that You are with me and for me, and You will never leave. In Jesus' name. Amen.*

Psalm 11

Life gets busy, and it's often hard to find time to rest, step away from the hustle and bustle, and calm your heart. When you struggle to find peace, remember the promises in tonight's verse: The Lord's eyes see everything; He examines everyone's actions. Nothing gets by His watch over you, and, as long as you seek Him, you will see His face.

There may be times you're tempted to flee your problems or look elsewhere for comfort. But tonight, you can feel His embrace and be filled with His strength as you take refuge in Him. Focusing on God's truth can put your mind at ease and allow your soul to rest peacefully. So as you close your eyes, open your heart to Him and listen for His voice. Put your fears and doubts in His hands and allow His presence to soothe your soul and lead you into His peace. Take comfort in the following verses and claim them as your own.

> *In the LORD I have taken shelter.*
> *How can you say to me,*
> *"Flee to a mountain like a bird.*
> *For look, the wicked prepare their bows,*
> *they put their arrows on the strings,*
> *to shoot in the darkness at the morally upright.*
> *When the foundations are destroyed,*
> *what can the godly accomplish?"*
> *The LORD is in His holy temple;*
> *the LORD's throne is in heaven.*
> *His eyes watch;*
> *His eyes examine all people.*
> *The LORD approves of the godly,*
> *but He hates the wicked and those who love to do violence....*
> *Certainly the LORD is just;*
> *He rewards godly deeds.*
> *The upright will experience His favor.*

PSALM 11:1–5, 7 NET

ADORATION: As you lie still, focus on the truths the psalmist reveals about God and worship Him for who He is. Reflect on His power and righteousness, and be reminded of His love for you.

Imagine a foundation so sturdy that it can never be shaken in a storm, it can never crumble underneath your feet. Know the Lord is your foundation that can never be shaken. Rest in the Lord's mighty hands and feel His protection surrounding you now, keeping you safe and secure through the night.

CONFESSION: Think of an uncertain time in your life when you tried to solve a problem or work out a struggle on your own instead of asking God for help. Confess when you've felt God wasn't big enough to handle your circumstances. Ask Him to help you now to rely on Him for everything you need.

THANKSGIVING: Praise God for the times He has protected you in your life. Praise God for the times He has provided for you and your friends and family. Thank Him for all the amazing things He is doing in your life right now and give Him all the glory.

SUPPLICATION: *Jesus, my Lord, I am afflicted and in need of Your presence and Your help. I claim Your promise to uphold me during times of persecution and hold on to the trust I have in Your power and strength. Guard my heart and remind me of the firm foundation I have in You no matter what I face. I love You and rest in Your arms tonight. Please bless me with the peace that is mine when I surrender my life to You. In Your great name, I pray. Amen.*

Psalm 12

Words have power. They can build us up, or they can destroy us. They can fill us with empty flattery, or they can speak truth into our lives. Sometimes it's hard to discern between what we hear and read as being true or false, but the Bible reminds us that God's Word is pure. The promises we have from Him never change. They are a safe haven to cling to for guidance and protection, for stability and assurance.

As you read the following Scripture, let God's heart soak into the recesses of yours. He loves you and cares for you, and He'll watch over you tonight.

> Help, LORD, for no faithful one remains;
> the loyal have disappeared from the human race.
> They lie to one another;
> they speak with flattering lips and deceptive hearts.
> May the LORD cut off all flattering lips
> and the tongue that speaks boastfully.
> They say, "Through our tongues we have power;
> our lips are our own—who can be our master?"
> "Because of the devastation of the needy
> and the groaning of the poor,
> I will now rise up," says the LORD.
> "I will provide safety for the one who longs for it."
> The words of the LORD are pure words,
> like silver refined in an earthen furnace,
> purified seven times.
> You, LORD, will guard us;
> You will protect us from this generation forever.
> The wicked prowl all around,
> and what is worthless is exalted by the human race.

PSALM 12 CSB

ADORATION: As you meditate on God's Word tonight, quiet all the noise in your mind and focus on His voice. Be still and focus on God's faithfulness to you. He has led you through every hard moment or season in life and brought you to the other side. And He will continue to do so. He will never leave you or turn away from you; you can completely trust in Him. He is worthy to be praised.

CONFESSION: Confess any lies you have believed before taking the time to test them against God's promises. Acknowledge any hurtful words you have spoken that have caused others to be discouraged. Ask the Lord to forgive you for any pain you have brought on yourself, as well as onto others. Ask Him to help you believe what He says about you and to think before you speak.

THANKSGIVING: Praise God for the loving words He has spoken over you and the ways they have brought life into your soul. Praise Him for the ways He provides for you, loves you, and is faithful to you. Thank Him for His unchanging Word and the reassurance that can be found there.

SUPPLICATION: *Father, thank You for Your Word and how it is a constant help at my disposal. I'm grateful for the wisdom, guidance, and reminders of Your love that are mine as I read Psalms. Remind me to go to Your Word for insight, good judgment, and truth before I listen to the voices of this world. Help me to use Your words to guard my mouth so that I will speak life and truth into others in order to lift them up and point them to You. In Your Son's name, I pray. Amen.*

Psalm 13

In the silence of the night when your mind is not distracted from the day, it is easy to feel anxious and replay moments of stress or regret in your mind. In these moments, there is comfort and strength in God's Word to remind you that He will deliver you from whatever you face—your heart will once again rejoice.

As you relax and settle your body down, close your eyes and quiet your mind. Breathe deeply and exhale the stresses of today. Focus on the greatness of God and the tender love He has for you. He has been faithful in the past, and He will be faithful to you now. Allow your thoughts to rest in knowing it is okay to cry out to God with all that's on your heart. He wants to hear from you; He is ready to receive your burdens. This psalm brings this to light with these beautiful, heartfelt cries to which we can all relate.

> How long, LORD? Will You forget me forever?
>   How long will You hide Your face from me?
> How long must I wrestle with my thoughts
>   and day after day have sorrow in my heart?
>   How long will my enemy triumph over me?
> Look on me and answer, LORD my God.
>   Give light to my eyes, or I will sleep in death,
> and my enemy will say, "I have overcome him,"
>   and my foes will rejoice when I fall.
> But I trust in Your unfailing love;
>   my heart rejoices in Your salvation.
> I will sing the LORD's praise,
>   for He has been good to me.

PSALM 13

ADORATION: No matter what difficulties we face, we can take delight in God's Word. It is trustworthy and reassuring, especially when life doesn't make sense. Worship the Lord for the gift of comfort we have when we read His loving words to us. Praise Him for reminding us that we are not alone—He is with us every step of our way—and we can rest assured that His timing and His ways are perfect.

CONFESSION: Think of a time when you struggled with waiting on God's timing and you took matters into your own hands, when you looked to the things of this world to give you joy and satisfaction. Ask God to help you be patient and wait for His timing. He will help you find joy in Him alone.

THANKSGIVING: Praise God for the prayers He has answered in your past. Praise Him for all the good things that make your life rich and meaningful now. Thank God for the gift of eternal life He freely offers to you today.

SUPPLICATION: *Father, I'm so comforted to know I can always turn to You when my heart is troubled and anxious thoughts overtake me. I cast them into Your hands now and ask that You hear my cry for help. Give me patience to wait on You to act on my behalf and to guide me one day at a time in the way You have for me. Protect me tonight; cover me with Your tender loving care. In Jesus' name. Amen.*

Psalm 14

Imagine a parent who sees that their child needs help, but they refuse to ask for it. Instead, they continue to try to do something themselves, to fall into frustration, and maybe even break down and cry. This is only a small glimpse of what God goes through as He waits for us, His children, to turn to Him for the help we need and the answers we're looking for. The Bible tells us we can take refuge in the Lord because His plans are never thwarted. His plans for us are good.

Tonight, as you finish processing the day, release any anxieties that linger. Take a deep breath and determine to look to God, who is watching over you. Seek His voice. Call on Him and wait for His reply. He is waiting patiently to pour His love out to you.

As you prepare to meditate on God's Word, ask Him to reveal His truth for your exact circumstances, and He will.

> Fools say to themselves,
>   "There is no God."...
> The LORD looked down from heaven on all people
>   to see if anyone understood,
>   if anyone was looking to God for help.
> But all have turned away.
>   Together, everyone has become evil.
> There is no one who does anything good,
>   not even one.
> Don't the wicked understand?
> They destroy my people as if they were eating bread.
>   They do not ask the LORD for help....
> The wicked upset the plans of the poor,
>   but the LORD will protect them.
> I pray that victory will come to Israel from Mount Zion!
>   May the LORD bring them back.
> Then the people of Jacob will rejoice,
>   and the people of Israel will be glad.

PSALM 14:1-4, 6-7 NCV

ADORATION: Tonight, as you lie down to sleep, reflect on God's loving presence and hold on to the hope that is yours as His child. Worship Him for being a refuge and an ever-present help who waits expectantly for you to turn to Him.

CONFESSION: Think of a time when you doubted God's reassuring presence. Confess that He is Lord and ask for His forgiveness. Now receive His forgiveness He loves to offer you.

THANKSGIVING: Praise God for revealing His truth in your life and thank Him for His patience and kindness toward you. Praise Him for the obstacles in your life that He has helped you overcome as you have called to Him and depended on Him for help.

SUPPLICATION: *Lord, thank You for Your patience during times I've not sought You with my whole heart for answers I've needed. I seek You now and ask that You help me maneuver any obstacles that are preventing me from moving forward with Your purpose for me. Help me to obey the commands from Your Word, and give me the wisdom I need for overcoming the hurdles I am facing now. I love You and praise Your holy name. Amen.*

Psalm 15

Y ou have been chosen by God to do amazing things through Him and for Him. So that you are best equipped for this life, He gives guidance in His Word for how to live so you can dwell on a solid foundation. As you read God's Word tonight, focus on the steps He invites you to take to follow Him and remain strong and secure as you go through life. Allow His truth to transform you from the inside out and surrender your ways to the righteous way He has for you.

As you close your eyes and wind down from the day, open your mind and heart to His voice. As you draw close to Him, let yourself feel His Spirit all around and the love He has for you. Allow these truths to speak to your heart and comfort you as you lie down to sleep.

> LORD, who may dwell in Your sacred tent?
> Who may live on Your holy mountain?
> The one whose walk is blameless,
> who does what is righteous,
> who speaks the truth from their heart;
> whose tongue utters no slander,
> who does no wrong to a neighbor,
> and casts no slur on others;
> who despises a vile person
> but honors those who fear the LORD;
> who keeps an oath even when it hurts,
> and does not change their mind;
> who lends money to the poor without interest;
> who does not accept a bribe against the innocent.
> Whoever does these things
> will never be shaken.
>
> **PSALM 15**

ADORATION: As you meditate on God's truth tonight, worship Him for His wisdom that will lead you through the ups and downs of life. Take comfort in knowing, as you follow His ways, you will find peace and joy, and renewal and refreshment for your mind, body, and spirit. Know that, as you follow His ways, you can transform the world around you. Rest knowing you will wake up in a better world because of God's presence in your life.

CONFESSION: Reflect on His commands in this psalm. Confess any that are a struggle for you to keep and any times when you were more concerned with the ways of this world than the ways of God. Ask God to help you value Him and His Word above all else.

THANKSGIVING: Praise God for His wisdom and guidance! Thank Him for leading you to the path of life. Praise Him for His righteousness, that being honorable and good are a part of who He is.

SUPPLICATION: *Lord, I cast all my cares on You tonight and relish this time to spend in the comfort of Your arms. Help me to release the things I'm trying to control and, instead, do things Your way. Help me to walk in Your way so that I can be victorious and strong no matter what I face. In Jesus' name. Amen.*

Psalm 16

Tonight, clear your mind and think about who you are to God—a child of His whom He dearly loves. He takes delight in you and cares for you. He wants to alleviate your stress and give you rest. Soak in the truth that He is the One who makes your life secure and fills it with good things.

As you relax, breathe in His goodness; breathe out your worry and receive the joy, the hope, and the safe, secure path that is yours when you embrace the following words as your own.

> Keep me safe, my God,
> for in You I take refuge.
> I say to the LORD, "You are my Lord;
> apart from You I have no good thing.". . .
> LORD, You alone are my portion and my cup;
> You make my lot secure.
> The boundary lines have fallen for me in pleasant places;
> surely I have a delightful inheritance.
> I will praise the LORD, who counsels me;
> even at night my heart instructs me.
> I keep my eyes always on the LORD.
> With Him at my right hand, I will not be shaken.
> Therefore my heart is glad and my tongue rejoices;
> my body also will rest secure,
> because You will not abandon me to the realm of the dead,
> nor will You let Your faithful one see decay.
> You make known to me the path of life;
> You will fill me with joy in Your presence,
> with eternal pleasures at Your right hand.

PSALM 16:1–2; 5–11

ADORATION: Close your eyes and reflect on all the ways that God works on your behalf, as mentioned in this psalm. Feel His love and delight enter every fiber of your being, bringing nourishment to your bones and rest to your flesh. Imagine how joyous and wonderful it will be to spend eternity walking with God, praising Him and loving Him forever.

CONFESSION: Reflect on the psalmist's words and any area of your life where you've not felt God's presence. Ask Him to help you value Him and His Word above all else, believing that what He says is true. Breathe in His forgiveness and grace. As you exhale, let go of your guilt and shame. Surrender to God's love and find inner peace and rest.

THANKSGIVING: As you surrender your heart to God once more, take delight in the Lord and His goodness. Allow His joy and His promises to gladden and reassure you. Rejoice in His wonderful name.

Praise God for the times He has protected you. Praise Him for guiding you, walking alongside you, and filling you with joyous hope and peaceful rest.

SUPPLICATION: *Father, You are my cup of blessing, and I praise You. Because of You, my heart is filled with peace in knowing You are with me—You even instruct me at night while I sleep. Let Your truth fill my soul with hope. Nourish my body as I rest and sleep in Your loving care. Help me to receive the abundant joy that is mine when I walk in Your ways. All praise be to You. Amen.*

Psalm 17

We all face circumstances or seasons of life that are tough, and it seems like we can't catch a break. Even in these moments, we can know that we are not alone—God is our Defender. He protects us; He fights our battles for us; He is our refuge and very present help in trouble.

As you wind down the day, imagine God between you and your opposition, your struggle, or your difficult circumstance. See Him as your shield. Release Him to fight on your behalf however He chooses. Trust in His promise to vindicate your cause and protect you while He does.

As you will see from the following verses, He is but a prayer away. He is your shelter that will not break, your anchor to keep you on stable ground.

> Hear me, LORD, my plea is just;
>   listen to my cry. . . .
> Let my vindication come from You;
>   may Your eyes see what is right. . . .
> I call on You, my God, for You will answer me;
>   turn Your ear to me and hear my prayer. . . .
> Keep me as the apple of your eye;
>   hide me in the shadow of Your wings
> from the wicked who are out to destroy me,
>   from my mortal enemies who surround me. . . .
> Their mouths speak with arrogance.
> They have tracked me down, they now surround me,
>   with eyes alert, to throw me to the ground. . . .
> Rise up, LORD, confront them, bring them down;
>   with Your sword rescue me from the wicked.
> By Your hand save me from such people, LORD, . . .
> May what You have stored up for the wicked fill their bellies; . . .
> As for me, I will be vindicated and will see Your face;
>   when I awake, I will be satisfied with seeing Your likeness.

PSALM 17:1–2, 6, 8–11, 13–15

ADORATION: The psalmist reminds us we are not alone as we go through life—we have an Advocate who protects our cause and provides calm for our minds. Worship Him in all His splendor for this promise and for how we can rely on Him in all ways—He has no limits to what He will do.

CONFESSION: Ask God to examine your heart and reveal any worry and fear in your life. Pray for His peace and His forgiveness. Breathe in His mercy and grace. As you exhale, let go of your guilt and shame. Surrender to God's love and find inner peace and rest.

THANKSGIVING: Rejoice in the Lord and His strength. Praise Him for His protection, for keeping you safe and secure through the night. Praise Him for being your refuge in times of trouble.

SUPPLICATION: *Father, I'm so comforted to know that You are watching over me tonight. I claim Your protection over my life and thank You for the safety and security I have in You. Renew my mind and body and give me Your strength to remain unmoved in spite of any difficult circumstances I face. In You I put my trust. Amen.*

Psalm 18

In this world, there are many troubles, but with the Lord's strength and power, you can overcome any obstacle you face. He promises to deliver you through your troubles. Tonight, draw near to the Lord with expectation—that He is present, He hears your prayers, He knows your need, He loves to rescue those He loves, and He loves you. Meditate on His strength now as you let these words from the psalms penetrate into the depths of your heart, knowing He will protect you and keep you secure through this night.

I love you, LORD, my strength.
The Lord is my rock, my fortress and my deliverer;
   my God is my rock, in whom I take refuge,
   my shield and the horn of my salvation, my stronghold.
I called to the LORD, who is worthy of praise,
   and I have been saved from my enemies. . . .
In my distress I called to the LORD;
   I cried to my God for help.
From His temple He heard my voice;
   my cry came before Him, into His ears. . . .
He reached down from on high and took hold of me;
   He drew me out of deep waters. . . .
You, LORD, keep my lamp burning;
   my God turns my darkness into light.
With Your help I can advance against a troop;
   with my God I can scale a wall. . . .
It is God who arms me with strength
   and keeps my way secure.
He makes my feet like the feet of a deer;
   He causes me to stand on the heights.
He trains my hands for battle;
   my arms can bend a bow of bronze.
You make your saving help my shield,
   and Your right hand sustains me;
   Your help has made me great. . . .
The LORD lives! Praise be to my Rock!
   Exalted be God my Savior!

PSALM 18:1-3, 6, 16, 28-29, 32-35, 46

ADORATION: Imagine being filled with God's strength in the same way the psalmist is, enabling you to climb mountains, hike treacherous paths, and cross tumultuous waters. His strength can help you overcome any challenges you are facing. Worship Him for being the great and holy God that He is and for His unfailing love and faithfulness in your life.

CONFESSION: We've all had times when we've doubted God's strength and power over a certain situation or struggle. Think of such a time when you doubted the power of God. Acknowledge you cannot face this world alone and you need His help.

THANKSGIVING: As you acknowledge the Lord's power, thank Him for His strength. Praise Him for being your rock and shield to sustain you and protect you through the night. Praise Him for being your fortress, surrounding you with His protection as you sleep.

SUPPLICATION: *Father, thank You for hearing me when I call on You for help. I ask that You be close to me. May I feel Your strength and power behind and before me. Be my strong foundation and fill my spirit and mind with renewed hope and faith through this night and into a new day. Cover me with Your peace and hold me as I rest assured that Your promises are true—I can completely trust in You. In Your great Son's name, I pray. Amen.*

Psalm 19

The Bible tells us all of creation testifies to the greatness of God. Looking up at the heavens and gazing at God's beautiful creation around us can change our perspective on the stresses we face. That's because we switch from looking inward to gazing at the handiwork of God that ranges from the unknown heights of the universe to the smallest reach of our fingertips. God is so great and vast, He is bigger than anything we face, yet He cares for His creation down to the smallest detail.

Tonight, close your eyes and meditate on the goodness of God. He is not only the Creator of the world but your creator. You bear His image and are a beautiful part of His creation. He is waiting to lift your burdens and give you rest. He wants to soothe your soul and renew your spirit with His truth. Allow tonight's psalm to bring the peace that you long for.

The heavens declare the glory of God;
*   the skies proclaim the work of His hands.*
Day after day they pour forth speech;
*   night after night they reveal knowledge.*
They have no speech, they use no words;
*   no sound is heard from them.*
Yet their voice goes out into all the earth,
*   their words to the ends of the world. . . .*
The law of the LORD is perfect,
*   refreshing the soul.*
The statutes of the LORD are trustworthy,
*   making wise the simple.*
The precepts of the LORD are right,
*   giving joy to the heart.*
The commands of the LORD are radiant,
*   giving light to the eyes. . . .*
The decrees of the LORD are firm,
*   and all of them are righteous.*
They are more precious than gold,
*   than much pure gold;*
they are sweeter than honey,

than honey from the honeycomb. . . .
May these words of my mouth and this meditation of my heart
  be pleasing in Your sight,
LORD, my Rock and my Redeemer.

PSALM 19:1-4, 7-10, 14

ADORATION: Contemplate the wonderful work of God's hands in creation. Thing about the beauty of the stars against the night sky and the brilliance of the sun's rays touching the earth as it travels from morning to evening. In the same way, His brilliance shines upon you, keeping you warm and safe. Praise Him for the work of His hands.

CONFESSION: Invite God to search your heart and examine your ways. Ask God to help you keep His commands. Surrender to the peace He gives when you confess and repent.

THANKSGIVING: Rejoice in the name of the Lord. Praise Him for the wonderful works He has done and for the beautiful creation He has made. Praise Him for His goodness in all of creation.

SUPPLICATION: *Father, Your creation is so amazing! Let me not go through a day without noticing Your beautiful handiwork and design in the world around me. Enlarge my heart to appreciate the love You've expressed through the wonders in nature and in me. I now rest in You tonight—all glory to You. Amen.*

Psalm 20

King David experienced victory after victory because he placed his confidence in God, not himself. In tonight's psalm, you can be inspired and encouraged to do the same. When you place your confidence in Him, He will help you rise above your circumstances and bring joy and hope to your heart.

As you tune out the busyness and troubles of the day, allow your mind to move into the peace and rest of God. Release your worries and your fears. Trust that He will be your strength. Call to Him with your cares and know that He will deliver you through them all.

May the LORD answer you when you are in distress;
may the name of the God of Jacob protect you.
May He send you help from the sanctuary
and grant you support from Zion.
May He remember all your sacrifices
and accept your burnt offerings.
May He give you the desire of your heart
and make all your plans succeed.
May we shout for joy over your victory
and lift up our banners in the name of our God.
May the LORD grant all your requests.
Now this I know:
The LORD gives victory to His anointed.
He answers him from His heavenly sanctuary
with the victorious power of His right hand.
Some trust in chariots and some in horses,
but we trust in the name of the LORD our God.
They are brought to their knees and fall,
but we rise up and stand firm.
LORD, give victory to the king!
Answer us when we call!

PSALM 20

ADORATION: You can find joy and peace as you prepare for sleep tonight, knowing the Lord will give you victory and peace over your troubles. Imagine Him holding you up with the power of His right hand, not letting any of your troubles or worries reach you. Worship Him for tonight's promises of deliverance; linger in praise for who He is.

CONFESSION: Let your heart lead you to truth and confess any struggles with trusting God. Ask Him to forgive you and to renew your faith in Him. Be filled with His mercy and grace, and surrender to the inner peace and rest you have in Him.

THANKSGIVING: Rejoice in His name. Praise God for the times He has helped you overcome difficult circumstances. Praise Him for the times He has delivered you from these trials. Praise Him for the times He has answered your prayers and you have seen victory.

SUPPLICATION: *Lord, I search my heart now and release to You my fear anxiety found there. Help me to completely trust and believe that You will deliver me from these fears as You work on my behalf. Give me the confidence that is mine when I walk in Your way. Give me Your joy and peace through this night as I rest in Your loving arms. In Your holy name, I pray. Amen.*

Psalm 21

No matter what your day looks like, no matter what obstacles are in front of us, there is joy to be found here—yes, joy! We can have joy because of God's strength that empowers us—to help us, to guard us, to hold us, and to lead us to victory and rest. We will not face a single struggle on our own, and this is something to celebrate.

As you breathe in the hope you have in God, breathe out the stresses you carry. Open your heart to His love and allow Him to usher you into His peace and calm. Tonight, find rest in the goodness and faithfulness of God, and let these verses lead you into the joy that is yours when your thoughts are focused on Him.

O LORD, the king rejoices in the strength You give;
he takes great delight in the deliverance You provide.
You grant him his heart's desire;
You do not refuse his request. (Selah)
For You bring him rich blessings;
You place a golden crown on his head.
He asked You to sustain his life,
and You have granted him long life and an enduring dynasty.
Your deliverance brings him great honor;
You give him majestic splendor.
For You grant him lasting blessings;
You give him great joy by allowing him into Your presence.
For the king trusts in the LORD,
and because of the Most High's faithfulness he is not shaken.
You prevail over all Your enemies;
Your power is too great for those who hate You.
You burn them up like a fiery furnace when You appear.
The LORD angrily devours them;
the fire consumes them.
You destroy their offspring from the earth,
their descendants from among the human race.
Yes, they intend to do You harm;
they dream up a scheme, but they do not succeed.
For You make them retreat

when You aim Your arrows at them.
Rise up, O LORD, in strength!
We will sing and praise Your power.

PSALM 21 NET

ADORATION: Worshiping God before you go to sleep can give you a new perspective of your day and help you focus on positive thoughts, calming your mind and relaxing your body. Reflect on His goodness and be reminded of His continual faithfulness of all the great things He has done, giving you deep, restful sleep.

CONFESSION: Think of a time when God granted your prayers and answered your request for something, but you were moving too quickly to realize He helped you and answered your pleas. Take a moment to acknowledge that and ask for His forgiveness and give Him the glory tonight!

THANKSGIVING: Rejoice in God's faithfulness. Praise God for the times He has answered your prayers and given you the desires of your heart. Praise Him for all the good things in your life.

SUPPLICATION: *Lord, I ask for healing of all the bruises I carry; restore my spirit and help me to remember Your mighty power. Surround me with Your soothing presence and receive my voice of praise for Your faithfulness to me. Thank You for loving me just as I am—let me rest in Your love tonight. Thank You for the gift of knowing that Your strength is mine to draw from in all the circumstances I face. In Jesus' name, I pray. Amen.*

Psalm 22

You are never alone. Jesus is here, and He wants to comfort you. As you settle down for the night, focus on your Savior. Think about how much He loved you in order to die for you on the cross, where His love was poured out for you. Know He understands the anguish you have felt in the past and the stress you are feeling tonight. He is ready to carry your burdens and replace them with His peace and hope. Open your heart to hear God's voice. Ask for His Word to restore your soul as you focus on the wonderful plans He has for your future.

> My God, my God, why have You forsaken me?
>   Why are You so far from saving me,
>   so far from my cries of anguish?
> My God, I cry out by day, but You do not answer,
>   by night, but I find no rest. . . .
> All who see me mock me;
>   they hurl insults, shaking their heads. . . .
> Yet You brought me out of the womb;
>   You made me trust in You, even at my mother's breast. . . .
> Do not be far from me,
>   for trouble is near
>   and there is no one to help. . . .
> My heart has turned to wax;
>   it has melted within me. . . .
> But You, LORD, do not be far from me.
>   You are my strength; come quickly to help me. . . .
> You who fear the LORD, praise Him! . . .
> For He has not despised or scorned
>   the suffering of the afflicted one;
> He has not hidden His face from him
>   but has listened to his cry for help. . . .
> All the ends of the earth
>   will remember and turn to the LORD,
> and all the families of the nations
>   will bow down before Him,

for dominion belongs to the LORD
and He rules over the nations.

PSALM 22:1-2, 7, 9, 11, 14, 19, 23-24, 27-28

ADORATION: Imagine a time when there will be no troubles, no stress, no worries, no suffering—a time when everyone will bow before the Lord and worship Him. What a joyful time that will be, as we all praise the Lord together! Allow that thought to lighten your heart and ease your mind. Rest in His presence and allow His love for you, as evidenced by His sacrifice on the cross, to be real to you tonight.

CONFESSION: Think of a time when you were in need and God seemed so far away from you. Confess any anger you had toward Him and allow His forgiveness to soften your heart. Remind yourself once more that He is always there for you, even when you can't feel Him nearby.

THANKSGIVING: Rejoice in God's faithfulness. Praise God for the times He has delivered you from your troubles. Praise Him for suffering on your behalf so that you may experience His joy, love, and grace tonight as you lie down to sleep.

SUPPLICATION: *Father, I turn my heart to You tonight and call out to You for help. I give You my fears and anxiety. I ask that You deliver me from all the "what ifs" that try to take over my thoughts. Help me recall the times You've been faithful to provide and bless my way. Give me peaceful rest through this night. I trust in You, O Lord. Amen.*

Psalm 23

Tonight, the Lord, your Shepherd, is with you, ready to guide you through His Word, ready to comfort you as you lie down to sleep. He knows you, He cares for you, and He loves you beyond compare. Picture yourself as one of His sheep looking to Him for protection and peace. Believe that He can and will give you everything you need to find rest tonight as you surrender to Him. Allow His voice to soothe your soul and guide you down a safe, secure path where you can find rest.

Psalm 23 describes the Lord as your Shepherd. Tonight, lean on Him and depend on Him to provide you protection and peace as you sleep.

The LORD is my shepherd;
I shall not want.
He makes me to lie down in green pastures;
He leads me beside the still waters.
He restores my soul;
He leads me in the paths of righteousness
For His name's sake.
Yea, though I walk through the valley of the shadow of death,
I will fear no evil;
For You are with me;
Your rod and Your staff, they comfort me.
You prepare a table before me in the presence of my enemies;
You anoint my head with oil;
My cup runs over.
Surely goodness and mercy shall follow me
All the days of my life;
And I will dwell in the house of the LORD
Forever.

PSALM 23 NKJV

ADORATION: A shepherd is responsible for providing, guiding, and protecting their sheep. We can rest assured that Jesus—our good Shepherd—does all this and more. Worship Him now not just for what He does, but for who He is. Because of Him, we can dwell in peace knowing we are safe throughout the night.

CONFESSION: Think about a time when you doubted the Lord's provision, guidance, and protection or were fearful. Ask for His forgiveness and put your trust in Him. Allow God's grace and love to be a comfort to you tonight.

THANKSGIVING: Rejoice in God's provision in your life. Think of all that He has given you and thank Him. Thank Him for the times He's comforted and cared for you.

SUPPLICATION: *Lord Jesus, thank You for how You've provided my needs, not just materially but emotionally and spiritually. Thank You for taking care of my needs even before I know I have a need. Guide me down safe paths and let me walk securely in You. Keep watch over me through this night and into a new day with You. In Your precious name, I pray. Amen.*

Psalm 24

As you wind down from the day, as you step away from the chaos and busy pace of life, step into God's loving embrace. You belong to Him; you are His child, and He cares for you. He isn't far off—He is with you now. The King of glory is with you to lift your burdens and listen to your cries. He sees what's on your heart and knows every detail of the circumstances around you.

Draw close and place your trust in Him. Seek to hear His voice as you read and meditate on His Word. Today's psalm explains that everything and everyone is the Lord's—that means you. Rest assured that God is holding you in His hands tonight.

> The earth is the LORD's, and everything in it,
>   the world, and all who live in it;
> for He founded it on the seas
>   and established it on the waters.
> Who may ascend the mountain of the LORD?
>   Who may stand in His holy place?
> The one who has clean hands and a pure heart,
>   who does not trust in an idol
>   or swear by a false god.
> They will receive blessing from the LORD
>   and vindication from God their Savior.
> Such is the generation of those who seek Him,
>   who seek Your face, God of Jacob.
> Lift up your heads, you gates;
>   be lifted up, you ancient doors,
>   that the King of glory may come in.
> Who is this King of glory?
>   The LORD strong and mighty,
>   the LORD mighty in battle.
> Lift up your heads, you gates;
>   lift them up, you ancient doors,
>   that the King of glory may come in.
> Who is He, this King of glory?

The LORD Almighty—
He is the King of glory.

PSALM 24

ADORATION: When the world doesn't make sense, the Bible tells us to take comfort in knowing the world is the Lord's and everything in it is His. Tonight, be reminded of the glory of the Creator. Worship Him for His lordship over your life and the protective covering He gives. No one and nothing can rule over you except Him—He is the Almighty God.

CONFESSION: Think of a time when you worshiped something or someone other than God. Confess any of these idols you are still holding on to and ask for His forgiveness. Ask God to help you put Him above all else in your life.

THANKSGIVING: Rejoice in God's sovereignty, that He is powerful and has authority. Rejoice in the wonderful work of His hands. Thank Him for what He has given you. Thank Him for the creation He made to provide for you.

SUPPLICATION: *Father, all I have is from You. You provide the very breath in my lungs. All good things in my life come from You. You are the King of glory, and I love You. Help me not to take the beauty of Your creation for granted; show me how to be a good steward of the blessings You pour over me. Keep me through this night and fill me with the kind of peace that only comes from You. I give You all the glory due Your name. In Jesus' name, I pray. Amen.*

Psalm 25

In tonight's psalm, David comes before God in complete honesty, saying he is "lonely and afflicted" (v. 16). Those are feelings to which we can all relate. But in reality, we are never alone—the Lord's compassion and faithful love are with us every moment of every day and night. Because of this, we can find the rest we need as we dwell in His presence.

As you close your eyes and turn from the events of the day, breathe in His breath of life, and breathe out the stresses you carry. Turn your heart and mind toward Jesus and rest in His arms. Relinquish your burdens to Him. Listen for His voice of love toward you. In Him, you can put your trust and know you are safe in His care.

> In you, LORD my God,
>> I put my trust.
> I trust in You;
>> do not let me be put to shame,
>> nor let my enemies triumph over me.
> No one who hopes in You
>> will ever be put to shame, . . .
> Show me Your ways, LORD,
>> teach me Your paths.
> Guide me in Your truth and teach me,
>> for You are God my Savior,
>> and my hope is in You all day long.
> Remember, LORD, Your great mercy and love,
>> for they are from of old. . . .
> All the ways of the LORD are loving and faithful
>> toward those who keep the demands of His covenant.
> For the sake of Your name, LORD,
>> forgive my iniquity, though it is great. . . .
> The LORD confides in those who fear Him;
>> He makes His covenant known to them.
> My eyes are ever on the LORD,
>> for only He will release my feet from the snare.
> Turn to me and be gracious to me,

for I am lonely and afflicted.
Relieve the troubles of my heart
   and free me from my anguish. . . .
Guard my life and rescue me;
   do not let me be put to shame,
   for I take refuge in You.
May integrity and uprightness protect me,
   because my hope, LORD, is in You.

PSALM 25:1-6, 10-11, 14-17, 20-21

ADORATION: Allow God's goodness to seep into your soul; feel His love come over you. Worship Him for His faithful love; bask in His presence and peace. Rest in knowing that He is God, and He is watching over you.

CONFESSION: Think through your day and acknowledge any sins that come to mind, asking God to forgive you. Pray for Him to take away your guilt and shame.

THANKSGIVING: Thank God for being trustworthy and for bringing you hope. Thank Him for being your Redeemer and giving you good gifts. Thank Him for the times He has protected you and delivered you.

SUPPLICATION: *Heavenly Father, teach me Your ways and guide me on a secure path where I will be safe. I want to hear Your voice and be in the center of Your will for my life. Be my refuge and strength, an ever-present help in my times of need. Help me to remember the unending love You have for me and that I can rest in it with my whole heart. I praise You and give You glory. Amen.*

Psalm 26

Every day we can find ourselves in situations where we could become frustrated with elements of our relationships with others. There could be the temptation to retaliate toward someone for hurt they've caused or frustration for the energy they bring to the relationship. But because of God's Spirit within us, we can find strength to remain patient and kind, acting toward others with integrity. Our praise for His wonderful works can ever be on our lips, knowing full well that God will listen to our feelings and work on our behalf. He frees us to remain in His glory, which brings much needed respite for our souls.

As you release the day, fall into the peace that is yours when you focus on the Savior. He longs for you to come, to rest, and to be in His presence. He knows every detail of your life. His truth is your shield, and your praise toward Him keeps your heart at peace as you sleep.

> Declare me innocent, O LORD,
>> for I have acted with integrity;
>> I have trusted in the LORD without wavering.
> Put me on trial, LORD, and cross-examine me.
>> Test my motives and my heart.
> For I am always aware of Your unfailing love,
>> and I have lived according to Your truth.
> I do not spend time with liars
>> or go along with hypocrites.
> I hate the gatherings of those who do evil,
>> and I refuse to join in with the wicked.
> I wash my hands to declare my innocence.
>> I come to Your altar, O LORD,
> singing a song of thanksgiving
>> and telling of all Your wonders.
> I love Your sanctuary, LORD,
>> the place where Your glorious presence dwells.
> Don't let me suffer the fate of sinners.
>> Don't condemn me along with murderers.

Their hands are dirty with evil schemes,
and they constantly take bribes.
But I am not like that; I live with integrity.
So redeem me and show me mercy.
Now I stand on solid ground,
and I will publicly praise the LORD.

PSALM 26 NLT

ADORATION: Relying on God for our needs reminds us that He can do more than we can imagine for our good. He is a God of mercy and justice. He defends us against our enemies with His strength. Take delight in His faithfulness and unfailing love, along with His kindness toward you. Allow the fullness of God's glory to fill your mind. Praise His name and feel the joy lighten your heart and brighten your spirit.

CONFESSION: As you surrender to God, invite Him to examine your mind and heart. Ask Him to reveal any sins you have committed so that you may ask for forgiveness. Allow His mercy and love to wash over you. Know that God is not a God of shame.

THANKSGIVING: Think of a time when God has delivered you from an unfair situation. Praise Him for His justice. Praise Him for His faithfulness in your life.

SUPPLICATION: *Lord, I put the challenges I face into Your hands tonight. I will trust in Your wisdom and faithfulness to help me through my trials however You lead. Help me to keep my integrity intact and to remember that I am a living testimony of Your love and power and strength, and that is what's most important to You. I love You and rest in Your care now for a deep and peaceful sleep. All glory to You. Amen.*

Psalm 27

There are so many things to fear in life, and it's easy to feel overwhelmed and defeated. When we face these difficult emotions, however, we can turn to our God, who is a God of comfort. He is a stronghold that isn't moved by fear. And when we cling to Him, who or what is there to be afraid of? He is our Protector, our Redeemer, our Confidence. He is also our safe place to land when we lie down to renew our spirit and body at the end of each day.

Turn to Him now and receive His blessed presence all around you. Soak in these verses as your own and let them give you peace.

> The LORD is my light and my salvation—
>> whom shall I fear?
> The LORD is the stronghold of my life—
>> of whom shall I be afraid? . . .
> Though an army besiege me,
>> my heart will not fear; . . .
> For in the day of trouble
>> He will keep me safe in His dwelling;
> He will hide me in the shelter of His sacred tent
>> and set me high upon a rock.
> Then my head will be exalted
>> above the enemies who surround me;
> at His sacred tent I will sacrifice with shouts of joy; . . .
> Hear my voice when I call, LORD;
>> be merciful to me and answer me.
> My heart says of you, "Seek His face!"
>> Your face, LORD, I will seek. . . .
> Though my father and mother forsake me,
>> the LORD will receive me.
> Teach me Your way, LORD;
>> lead me in a straight path
>> because of my oppressors. . . .
> I remain confident of this:
>> I will see the goodness of the LORD

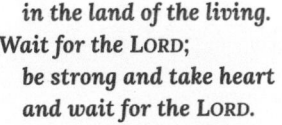

in the land of the living.
Wait for the LORD;
   be strong and take heart
   and wait for the LORD.

PSALM 27:1, 3, 5–8, 10–11, 13–14

ADORATION: Take a few moments to ponder the goodness of God as described in this psalm. Allow His hope to bring you comfort. Thank Him for the love you feel in your heart as He sustains you through this night.

CONFESSION: Think of a time when you did not place your confidence in God. Confess any doubts you have about His goodness and faithfulness. Ask God to help you be confident in Him tonight.

THANKSGIVING: Praise God for His help in the past, in the present, and for what He will do in your future. Thank Him for the never-ending hope He gives, even when you are dealing with overwhelm or defeat.

SUPPLICATION: *Lord, tonight I release myself and my fears into Your hands and draw my strength from You. Help me to live out the confidence You give no matter what I face. You are my Stronghold, my Help, and my Shelter. You won't abandon me—You will always be with me—and I am so grateful. Now please bless my sleep so I'm refreshed and renewed for a victorious day tomorrow. In Jesus' name, I pray. Amen.*

Psalm 28

The Bible tells us prayer is the most effective way to fight our battles. When we cry out to the Lord, we can trust Him to defend us, protect us, and sustain us through the night. And the good news is that there is no wrong way to pray. It is simply a matter of talking to God honestly from the heart. He hears every word we speak and releases His power to bring the help we need and the answers we are seeking.

Now take a moment to clear your mind and focus your thoughts on God. Acknowledge that He is your Rock that you can always count on to comfort you, sustain you, and uphold you through the night. He knows the weight of what you are carrying from today, and He is ready to lift your burdens and give you rest for your mind, body, and soul. Claim the promises in His Word as your own and rest in their truth.

To you, LORD, I call;
   You are my Rock,
   do not turn a deaf ear to me.
For if You remain silent,
   I will be like those who go down to the pit.
Hear my cry for mercy
   as I call to You for help,
as I lift up my hands
   toward your Most Holy Place.
Do not drag me away with the wicked,
   with those who do evil,
who speak cordially with their neighbors
   but harbor malice in their hearts.
Repay them for their deeds
   and for their evil work;
repay them for what their hands have done
   and bring back on them what they deserve.
Because they have no regard for the deeds of the LORD
   and what His hands have done,
He will tear them down
   and never build them up again.
Praise be to the LORD,

for He has heard my cry for mercy.
The LORD is my strength and my shield;
   my heart trusts in Him, and He helps me.
My heart leaps for joy,
   and with my song I praise Him.
The LORD is the strength of His people,
   a fortress of salvation for His anointed one.
Save Your people and bless Your inheritance;
   be their shepherd and carry them forever.

PSALM 28

ADORATION: Invite God's presence to be with you tonight as you sleep. Take delight in His hope. Take comfort in His strength. As His presence fills your room, feel your soul find rest. Know He will lift you and keep you upon His rock forever.

CONFESSION: Think of a time when you took matters into your own hands rather than turn to the Lord for His help and strength. Ask for His forgiveness as well as help with turning to Him first in the future.

THANKSGIVING: Praise God for all the ways He provides for you—as your help, your rescue, and your strength. Recall a time you felt the Lord's guidance in a tricky situation and the way He guided you through.

SUPPLICATION: *Father, be my stronghold and shield when I face opposition. Cover me with Your grace when I face trials. Be my Shepherd who carries me to safety in Your holy presence. In Your Son's great name, I pray. Amen.*

Psalm 29

One of the best things we can do is to stop and recognize God for who He is. When we ascribe to Him the posture of praise, we no longer focus on ourselves and the weight we carry, but on the worship He deserves as Creator of the universe.

Tonight, as you wind down from your day, quiet your mind and look to Him. He is your God. He created you; He loves you, and He wants to bless you with His presence. Let His voice speak into your soul—through prayer and meditation and through His Word. Let His promises to you speak louder than the concerns on your heart. Find rest in knowing He is your strength for life. He is your hope for eternity. And He is your peace for this night.

> Ascribe to the LORD, you heavenly beings,
>   ascribe to the LORD glory and strength.
> Ascribe to the LORD the glory due His name;
>   worship the LORD in the splendor of His holiness.
> The voice of the LORD is over the waters;
>   the God of glory thunders,
>   the LORD thunders over the mighty waters.
> The voice of the LORD is powerful;
>   the voice of the LORD is majestic.
> The voice of the LORD breaks the cedars;
>   the LORD breaks in pieces the cedars of Lebanon.
> He makes Lebanon leap like a calf,
>   Sirion like a young wild ox.
> The voice of the LORD strikes
>   with flashes of lightning.
> The voice of the LORD shakes the desert;
>   the LORD shakes the Desert of Kadesh.
> The voice of the LORD twists the oaks
>   and strips the forests bare.
> And in His temple all cry, "Glory!"
> The LORD sits enthroned over the flood;
>   the LORD is enthroned as King forever.

The LORD gives strength to His people;
the LORD blesses His people with peace.

PSALM 29

ADORATION: Meditate on the Lord's majesty and power, as described in today's psalm. Think about the fact that His voice is powerful enough to break cedars yet gentle enough to soothe your soul as you lie down to sleep. Allow His sovereignty, His power, and His gentleness to bring you hope for tomorrow and peace for tonight.

CONFESSION: Think of a time when you've allowed your circumstances to overshadow your praise and devotion to God. Confess any fears and doubts you have now that keep you from seeing Him and hearing His voice. Know He is always with you, and His power is always available to you.

THANKSGIVING: Think of a time when God's strength helped you face a difficult time in your life. Praise Him for how He is helping you now and the comfort that brings. Praise Him for His holy presence throughout your day and night, that His kind and loving nature is a part of who He is.

SUPPLICATION: *Father, I look to You with a heart full of love and thanksgiving for You. Thank You for watching over my life and for speaking into my heart in exactly the ways I need. Thank You for being my strength, for blessing me with Your peace. In Jesus' name, I pray. Amen.*

Psalm 30

The Bible reminds us that God doesn't prevent us from facing difficult circumstances, but He does promise to walk through them with us. He is a healing balm in the midst of our pain. When we cry out and release our fear and anxiety to Him, He's there to comfort and sustain us. We can have His joy with each new dawning day, no matter what our life looks like.

Tonight, as you draw near to Him, allow Him to turn your sorrow into joy, your stress into peace, your despair into hope, and your lament into dancing. Rest securely and know that He will hold you through the night as you sleep and renew your body and spirit.

I will exalt you, LORD,
because You have lifted me up
and have not allowed my enemies
to triumph over me.
LORD my God,
I cried to You for help, and You healed me.
LORD, You brought me up from Sheol;
You spared me from among those
going down to the Pit.
Sing to the LORD, you His faithful ones,
and praise His holy name.
For His anger lasts only a moment,
but His favor, a lifetime.
Weeping may stay overnight,
but there is joy in the morning.
When I was secure, I said,
"I will never be shaken."
LORD, when You showed Your favor,
You made me stand like a strong mountain;
when You hid Your face, I was terrified.
LORD, I called to You;
I sought favor from my LORD:
"What gain is there in my death,
if I go down to the Pit?

Will the dust praise You?
Will it proclaim Your truth?
LORD, listen and be gracious to me;
LORD, be my helper."
You turned my lament into dancing;
You removed my sackcloth
and clothed me with gladness,
so that I can sing to You and not be silent.
LORD my God, I will praise You forever.

PSALM 30 CSB

ADORATION: Know that God is your Helper. Think about the fact that He is here to help you, not harm you, and to give you joy and hope for tomorrow. Rejoice in His holy name! Allow His hope and peace to wash over you now and through this night.

CONFESSION: Think of a time when you found your security in your success in this world instead of in God's steadiness and His plan for your life. Ask Him to help you find your security in Him alone and not in anyone or anything of this world.

THANKSGIVING: Praise God for when you have felt His comfort and joy in the midst of difficulty. Praise Him for His faithfulness. Praise Him for His healing presence in your life.

SUPPLICATION: *Lord, listen and be gracious to me. I need You. I need Your help and Your healing through this night and into the morning. Help me to have Your joy regardless of my circumstances. Help me to hold on to the hope that You offer so freely. Help my heart to sing and be filled with Your favor. Restore my soul as I sleep and rest in Your arms. To You, I lift up my praise. Amen.*

Psalm 31

How wonderful it is to know that we have a safe haven—a refuge to conceal and protect us, to guard and to heal our hearts. When we trust God and look to Him for shelter, He promises to deliver His goodness, and that includes bestowing His blessing onto us.

As you bring your thoughts and feelings to God tonight, allow your mind and your heart to trust completely in Him. Imagine His presence filling your room, surrounding you with His mercy and love. Remember He is the all-powerful One who knows you, sees you, and sustains you through the night. He will never leave you nor forsake you. He will always be by your side.

As you read tonight's psalm, ask Him to speak to you through His Word and reveal His truth to you.

In You, LORD, I have taken refuge;
   let me never be put to shame;
   deliver me in your righteousness. . . .
Keep me free from the trap that is set for me,
   for You are my refuge.
Into Your hands I commit my spirit;
   deliver me, LORD, my faithful God. . . .
I will be glad and rejoice in Your love,
   for You saw my affliction
   and knew the anguish of my soul.
You have not given me into the hands of the enemy
   but have set my feet in a spacious place.
Be merciful to me, LORD, for I am in distress;
   my eyes grow weak with sorrow,
   my soul and body with grief. . . .
But I trust in You, LORD;
   I say, "You are my God."
My times are in Your hands;
   deliver me from the hands of my enemies,
   from those who pursue me. . . .
Love the LORD, all His faithful people!

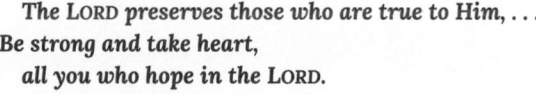

The LORD preserves those who are true to Him, . . .
Be strong and take heart,
   all you who hope in the LORD.

PSALM 31:1, 4-5, 7-9, 14-15, 23-24

ADORATION: God's Word can be a source of comfort for you tonight. Worship the Lord as your rock, your fortress, as One who upholds and protects you through the darkness of this night.

CONFESSION: Think of something or someone in your life that you have put in the place of God. Confess this to Him and ask for His forgiveness as you realign your priorities. Ask Him to help you worship Him only and to help you put Him above all else.

THANKSGIVING: Think of times when you've experienced God's faithfulness in difficulties and thank Him for His deliverance. Praise Him for being the One true source you can always count on.

SUPPLICATION: *Father, I can so often get overwhelmed by the circumstances and stressors in my life. I come to You now and ask You to be my refuge. Cover me with Your faithful love, and help me to be strong and courageous through the power that is mine through You. I praise You for being my rock, my fortress, and my deliverer, whom I can always trust. All glory be to You. Amen.*

Psalm 32

We all need forgiveness. Whether for a carelessly spoken word or an egregious act, unless we seek and receive forgiveness, we miss out on the blessing and freedom that forgiveness provides. Tonight's psalm focuses on God's forgiveness toward us and the joy that is ours when we walk in it. We don't have to carry the weight of guilt or shame that our transgressions can bring. Because of the Savior, each new breath we take fills us with His mercies and love.

Clear your mind now and open your heart to hear God's voice. Ask Him to speak to you through the following psalm. Find joy in God's forgiveness and allow it to lighten your heart, calm your mind, and relax your body.

Blessed is the one
   whose transgressions are forgiven,
   whose sins are covered.
Blessed is the one
   whose sin the LORD does not count against them
   and in whose spirit is no deceit.
When I kept silent,
   my bones wasted away
   through my groaning all day long.
For day and night
   Your hand was heavy on me;
my strength was sapped
   as in the heat of summer.
Then I acknowledged my sin to You
   and did not cover up my iniquity.
I said, "I will confess
   my transgressions to the LORD."
And You forgave
   the guilt of my sin.
Therefore let all the faithful pray to You
   while You may be found;
surely the rising of the mighty waters
   will not reach them.

You are my hiding place;
    You will protect me from trouble
    and surround me with songs of deliverance.
I will instruct you and teach you in the way you should go;
    I will counsel you with my loving eye on you. . . .
Many are the woes of the wicked,
    but the LORD's unfailing love
    surrounds the one who trusts in Him.
Rejoice in the LORD and be glad, you righteous;
    sing, all you who are upright in heart!

PSALM 32:1-8, 10-11

ADORATION: God's forgiveness is greater than our sin! He does not keep a record of our wrongs, and He is always ready to hear and forgive. Let's take delight in this promise and find joy and freedom in His forgiveness and love.

CONFESSION: Think of a time when you refused to follow God's way. Confess the sin that came from following your own path. Ask for His forgiveness and for His deliverance and commit your life into His care.

THANKSGIVING: Thank God for forgiving your transgressions and covering your sins. Praise Him for redeeming and restoring you. Rejoice in the Lord and be glad!

SUPPLICATION: *Lord, please soften my heart and show me any ways I've sinned against You today. Please forgive me and cleanse me from the weight I've carried because of it. Give me courage to work through the consequences that exist because of my sin and help me to keep looking to You for guidance and counsel for repair. Help me also to forgive myself and not hold on to any shame that tries to linger in my heart. Help me to fully receive and walk in Your grace. May I sleep peacefully tonight knowing that I am forgiven. In Jesus' name and power, I pray. Amen.*

Psalm 33

Not only did God create the universe and all that is in it, He watches over His creation the way a loving parent watches over his or her child. His Word says, "He gazes on all the inhabitants of the earth" (Psalm 33:13 CSB), which means His eyes are on you now. His ear is attentive to your prayers. His heart is full of love for you.

As you lie down to sleep, try to calm your mind. Bask in His presence and allow His truth to ease your mind and soothe your soul. Think on how much He cares for you—His creation. Know that His faithful love rests on you tonight as you put your trust in Him.

> Rejoice in the LORD, you righteous ones;
> praise from the upright is beautiful. . . .
> Sing a new song to Him;
> play skillfully on the strings, with a joyful shout.
> For the word of the LORD is right,
> and all His work is trustworthy.
> He loves righteousness and justice;
> the earth is full of the LORD's unfailing love.
> The heavens were made by the word of the LORD,
> and all the stars, by the breath of His mouth. . . .
> Happy is the nation whose God is the LORD—
> the people He has chosen to be His own possession!
> The LORD looks down from heaven;
> He observes everyone.
> He gazes on all the inhabitants of the earth
> from His dwelling place.
> He forms the hearts of them all;
> He considers all their works. . . .
> The LORD keeps His eye on those who fear Him—
> those who depend on His faithful love
> to rescue them from death
> and to keep them alive in famine.
> We wait for the LORD;
> He is our help and shield.
> For our hearts rejoice in Him
> because we trust in His holy name.

May your faithful love rest on us, LORD,
for we put our hope in You.

PSALM 33:1, 3-6, 12-15, 18-22 CSB

ADORATION: The same God who spoke the world into existence is the God who speaks truth and love into your life. Take time to delight in this amazing fact and let love for Him flow from your heart.

CONFESSION: Confess any times you have taken God's good gifts in your life for granted. Ask for His forgiveness and His help to remember His blessings, the majesty of the heavens, and the miracle of your life.

THANKSGIVING: Rejoice in His power and majesty that is on display in creation and in your life. Thank Him for His Word and for revealing His truth to you. Thank Him for the times He has helped you and delivered you through your troubles.

SUPPLICATION: *Father, thank You for the beauty of Your creation, which I so enjoy. Thank You for reassuring me that You see me, You know about the details of my life, and Your hand is on each one. Thank You for all the ways You've shown Your faithful love to me and the comfort that brings. You are so good to me. Let me always be mindful of that. In Jesus' name, I pray. Amen.*

Psalm 34

The Bible says blessed are those who take refuge in the Lord. So tonight, think about the things you need a refuge from. Is it overwhelming demands? Is it fear of failure? Is it the hurt from a loss? Now set your mind on God's promise to be your refuge in this time of need. Turn to Him with all your heart and surrender your burdens one by one to Him. Imagine each weight on your heart lifting up into His hands.

The Lord promises to deliver us from our troubles, to redeem what we consider lost. As you focus on His Word, embrace these promises as your own; look to Him and His love for you.

> I will bless the LORD at all times;
> His praise will always be on my lips. . . .
> Those who look to Him are radiant with joy;
> their faces will never be ashamed. . . .
> The angel of the LORD encamps
> around those who fear Him, and rescues them.
> Taste and see that the LORD is good.
> How happy is the person who takes refuge in Him!
> You who are His holy ones, fear the LORD,
> for those who fear Him lack nothing. . . .
> Those who seek the LORD
> will not lack any good thing. . . .
> The eyes of the LORD are on the righteous,
> and His ears are open to their cry for help. . . .
> The righteous cry out, and the LORD hears,
> and rescues them from all their troubles.
> The LORD is near the brokenhearted;
> He saves those crushed in spirit.
> One who is righteous has many adversities,
> but the LORD rescues him from them all.
> He protects all his bones;
> not one of them is broken. . . .
> The LORD redeems the life of His servants,
> and all who take refuge in Him will not be punished.

PSALM 34:1, 5, 7–10, 15, 17–20, 22 CSB

ADORATION: In the silence of the night, our troubles threaten to overwhelm us. But God's Word reminds us that we are not alone: He is with us and will be our refuge when we look to Him. He is our hope and peace and will ease our minds and calm our hearts. Worship Him now for this great promise.

CONFESSION: Confess the times when you've relied on your own strength to work through a trial rather than seek God for His refuge and help. Allow His grace to wash over you and remember there is no condemnation or shame in Christ.

THANKSGIVING: Praise the Lord for delivering you from your fears. Praise Him for His protection and provision in your life. Praise Him for His faithfulness to answer your prayers and intercede on your behalf.

SUPPLICATION: *Lord, I submit to You now the burdens I've been trying to carry on my own. I need Your shelter and the respite You provide. I look to You for my strength and the protection You give from the harmful elements of this world. Thank You for hearing my prayer and redeeming the time and energy I've lost. I love You and rest in Your care now and through this night. All praise be to You. Amen.*

Psalm 35

God tells us repeatedly throughout His Word not to be afraid of those who persecute us or who repay our good deeds with hurtful or careless ones. He makes it clear that He will vindicate us, defend us, and uphold us with His strength. We can't always see Him at work on our behalf, but we can trust that He is. Because of this, we can surrender to Him our thanksgiving and praise, knowing that the victory is already ours. We can rest in His very words, "He takes pleasure in His servant's well-being" (Psalm 35:27 CSB)—that is His desire for us.

As you end the day and turn your mind and thoughts onto God, it's okay to vent about all that troubles you, just as King David did. As you unburden your heart, you can then turn your thoughts to praise.

Oppose my opponents, LORD;
fight those who fight me.
Take Your shields—large and small—
and come to my aid.
Draw the spear and javelin against my pursuers,
and assure me, "I am your deliverance." . . .
Then I will rejoice in the LORD;
I will delight in His deliverance.
All my bones will say,
"LORD, who is like You,
rescuing the poor from one too strong for him,
the poor or the needy from one who robs him?"
Malicious witnesses come forward; . . .
They repay me evil for good,
making me desolate.
Yet when they were sick,
my clothing was sackcloth;
I humbled myself with fasting,
and my prayer was genuine. . . .
But when I stumbled, they gathered in glee;
they gathered against me. . . .
Wake up and rise to my defense,

to my cause, my God and my Lord!
Vindicate me, LORD my God,
in keeping with Your righteousness,
and do not let them rejoice over me....
Let those who want my vindication
shout for joy and be glad;
let them continually say,
"The LORD be exalted.
He takes pleasure in His servant's well-being."
And my tongue will proclaim Your righteousness,
Your praise all day long.

PSALM 35:1-3, 9-13, 15, 23-24, 27-28 CSB

ADORATION: God says we will be persecuted in this world, but the Lord will defend us and uphold us. He will fight our battles and give us victory if we surrender to Him. So, tonight, open your heart to His strength and justice imparted to you.

CONFESSION: Think of a time when you took up vengeance yourself against someone who was treating you unfairly or slandering your reputation. Confess any anger or resentment you have toward this person. Ask God to help you be patient and allow Him to avenge those who hurt you and persecute you.

THANKSGIVING: Thank the Lord for His love toward you, greater than you can even imagine. Praise Him for His righteousness and heart of justice. Thank Him for the times when He has rescued you and helped you in the midst of trouble.

SUPPLICATION: *Lord, it's hard not to retaliate when someone wrongs me. Help me to turn to You at once when I need Your defense for my cause. Help me to remember to call on You, that You are very near, and that You will help me. Remind me that I am Yours, my reputation is Yours, my life is Yours. You want my well-being. I praise You and love You for being my God. In Jesus' name. Amen.*

Psalm 36

In tonight's psalm, David contrasts the wickedness and brokenness of humanity with the goodness and holiness of our Lord. Even if the world seems to be a dark place, we can always find comfort in the light of the Lord. His light can extinguish the darkness that surrounds us, bringing joy, hope, and peace to our hearts.

As you focus your thoughts on God, take a deep breath and slow down your mind. Allow your spirit to align with His presence as you remember who He is—the holy, righteous One who knows you, loves you, and saves you. Listen for His voice and meditate on His faithfulness.

I have a message from God in my heart
concerning the sinfulness of the wicked:
There is no fear of God
before their eyes.
In their own eyes they flatter themselves
too much to detect or hate their sin.
The words of their mouths are wicked and deceitful;
they fail to act wisely or do good.
Even on their beds they plot evil;
they commit themselves to a sinful course
and do not reject what is wrong.
Your love, LORD, reaches to the heavens,
Your faithfulness to the skies.
Your righteousness is like the highest mountains,
Your justice like the great deep.
You, LORD, preserve both people and animals.
How priceless is Your unfailing love, O God!
People take refuge in the shadow of Your wings.
They feast on the abundance of Your house;
You give them drink from Your river of delights.
For with You is the fountain of life;
in Your light we see light.
Continue Your love to those who know You,
Your righteousness to the upright in heart.

> *May the foot of the proud not come against me,*
> *nor the hand of the wicked drive me away.*
> *See how the evildoers lie fallen—*
> *thrown down, not able to rise!*

PSALM 36

ADORATION: Take a moment now to exalt and praise the Lord for His goodness. Worship Him for His holy presence in your life. Devote your life once again to the One who gives light and life in a dark and fallen world. His loving-kindness is endless; His compassion is great.

CONFESSION: Think of a time when you did not reject what was wrong and followed the crowd. Ask for God's forgiveness for not looking to Him first and foremost. Ask Him to give you courage to stand for what is right and trust in His ways.

THANKSGIVING: Praise the Lord for His goodness, faithfulness, and justice. Praise Him for His unfailing love. Thank Him for His provision in your life.

SUPPLICATION: *Lord, there is so much injustice all around. I pray that Your justice will prevail in every difficult situation. Please intervene in unfair situations in my life. Help me turn to Your power and strength when confronted by malice or deception. You are my strong tower. I place my hope and trust in You as I close this day in Your loving presence. All glory be to You. Amen.*

Psalm 37

The Bible assures us that God sees everything, so when we are witness to evil and wrongdoing God knows what is transpiring as well. This is reassuring because His Word says He loves justice, and He will not abandon those He loves. He holds our hand and gives us His strength to keep walking in the way He leads.

Tonight, take a moment to exhale and surrender the day to God, then allow His love and peace to fill your mind and heart. Let go of your anxieties and your fears. Calm your mind as you take in God's truth in this psalm.

Do not be agitated by evildoers;
do not envy those who do wrong. . . .
Trust in the LORD and do what is good;
dwell in the land and live securely.
Take delight in the LORD,
and He will give you your heart's desires.
Commit your way to the LORD;
trust in Him, and He will act, . . .
Be silent before the LORD and wait expectantly for Him;
do not be agitated by one who prospers in his way,
by the person who carries out evil plans.
Refrain from anger and give up your rage;
do not be agitated—it can only bring harm. . . .
The LORD watches over the blameless all their days,
and their inheritance will last forever.
They will not be disgraced in times of adversity;
they will be satisfied in days of hunger. . . .
A person's steps are established by the LORD,
and He takes pleasure in his way.
Though he falls, he will not be overwhelmed,
because the LORD supports him with His hand. . . .
For the LORD loves justice
and will not abandon His faithful ones.
They are kept safe forever. . . .
Wait for the LORD and keep His way,
and He will exalt you to inherit the land.

You will watch when the wicked are destroyed. . . .
The salvation of the righteous is from the LORD,
their refuge in a time of distress.
The LORD helps and delivers them;
He will deliver them from the wicked and will save them
because they take refuge in Him.

PSALM 37:1, 3-5, 7-8, 18-19, 23-24, 28, 34, 39-40 CSB

ADORATION: Take some time to offer praise to God for His help and deliverance, as addressed in today's psalm; express to Him your delight and security in His presence.

CONFESSION: Has there been a time when you envied someone due to their wealth or success, or begrudged someone who succeeded while taking shortcuts? Confess any jealousy or resentment in your heart. Ask God for strength when a similar situation arises, and praise God for His provision for you.

THANKSGIVING: Thank God for the ways He has provided for you. Praise Him for His faithfulness. Thank Him for the ways He has blessed you.

SUPPLICATION: *Lord, I lift up the worries of this day to You. I release the wrongdoing I see into Your hands and trust You with the outcome. Give me patience as I wait on You to act on my behalf in my areas of need. Help me to still my mind so I can focus on Your truth. Lead me to rest in Your truth tonight. In Jesus' name, I pray. Amen.*

Psalm 38

God's Word tells us our sin and brokenness are a part of our story, but they are not the end of our story. God has a plan for our mistakes and failures. He redeems what we've lost and makes our crooked way straight. He works to restore what sin has broken. And there is no sin that will separate us from His love.

In this truth, we find deep, peaceful rest. There is renewed hope in confession and repentance, trusting the Lord will heal and protect those who bring their brokenness to Him. He knows the sins of our past, our present, and our future, yet He continues to pursue us; He is constantly drawing us near to Him through the presence of His Spirit. As you meditate on His Word tonight, open your heart to its truths that will bring you comfort.

> LORD, do not rebuke me in Your anger
> or discipline me in Your wrath.
> Your arrows have pierced me,
> and Your hand has come down on me.
> Because of Your wrath there is no health in my body;
> there is no soundness in my bones because of my sin.
> My guilt has overwhelmed me
> like a burden too heavy to bear.
> My wounds fester and are loathsome
> because of my sinful folly.
> I am bowed down and brought very low;
> all day long I go about mourning.
> My back is filled with searing pain;
> there is no health in my body.
> I am feeble and utterly crushed;
> I groan in anguish of heart. . . .
> My heart pounds, my strength fails me;
> even the light has gone from my eyes. . . .
> For I am about to fall,
> and my pain is ever with me.
> I confess my iniquity;
> I am troubled by my sin.
> Many have become my enemies without cause;

> *those who hate me without reason are numerous.*
> *Those who repay my good with evil*
>   *lodge accusations against me,*
>   *though I seek only to do what is good.*
> *LORD, do not forsake me;*
>   *do not be far from me, my God.*
> *Come quickly to help me,*
>   *my Lord and my Savior.*

PSALM 38:1-8, 10, 17-22

ADORATION: Imagine God's presence filling your room. He is with you, He is never far from you, and you never have to face any trouble, any fear, or any sin alone. Praise Him for not letting anything separate you from His love.

CONFESSION: Search your heart and speak any unconfessed sin before the Lord. Repent and ask God to transform your sorrow into joy. Receive the grace and love He has just for you.

THANKSGIVING: Thank God for His forgiveness. Thank Him for never giving up on you. Thank Him for the ways He has brought healing to your life.

SUPPLICATION: *Father God, I'm so grateful for second and third and fourth chances with You. Thank You for not leaving me in my sin. Thank You for covering me with cleansing and restoration and the peace and calm You give. I put my hope in You, Lord Jesus. Amen.*

Psalm 39

Society tells us that we will feel secure by collecting things, equating our possessions with our happiness and peace of mind. Yet God's Word tells us to find our security in Him because God has purposes for us far beyond what we gain for ourselves. When we seek Him, we become rich in heavenly possessions and in the security of knowing God as our Savior. Our priorities are realigned in light of eternity.

Breathe in and exhale the day. In your mind, let go of the things you think you need to be fulfilled and turn to God with your whole heart. As you meditate on the words from tonight's psalm, let Him be enough for you in this moment.

> I said, "I will guard my ways
> so that I may not sin with my tongue; . . .
> My heart grew hot within me;
> as I mused, a fire burned.
> I spoke with my tongue:
> "LORD, make me aware of my end
> and the number of my days
> so that I will know how short-lived I am.
> In fact, You have made my days just inches long,
> and my life span is as nothing to You.
> Yes, every human being stands as only a vapor. Selah
> Yes, a person goes about like a mere shadow.
> Indeed, they rush around in vain,
> gathering possessions
> without knowing who will get them.
> "Now, Lord, what do I wait for?
> My hope is in You.
> Rescue me from all my transgressions;
> do not make me the taunt of fools.
> I am speechless; I do not open my mouth
> because of what You have done. . . .
> "Hear my prayer, LORD,
> and listen to my cry for help;
> do not be silent at my tears.

For I am here with You as an alien,
a temporary resident like all my ancestors.
Turn Your angry gaze from me
so that I may be cheered up
before I die and am gone."

PSALM 39:1, 3–9, 12–13 CSB

ADORATION: Spend a few moments thinking on how perfectly God has planned out your life and how He desires what is best for you. Remember that His love for you will never perish, whereas material possessions will. Worship Him for the glory of His presence, which gives hope for lasting joy and life with Him.

CONFESSION: Think of a time when you put your hope in the things of this world, like wealth or professional success. Confess the things in your life you have put above God. Ask for God's forgiveness, knowing that true joy is found in aligning yourself with Him. Pray He will help you prioritize what's important to Him in your life.

THANKSGIVING: Thank God for the days He has given you in your life. Thank Him for the family and friends He has blessed you with. Thank Him for the good gifts He has given to you to enjoy.

SUPPLICATION: *Lord, I turn to You and ask that You deliver me from buying unnecessary things and planning my life for temporary gain. Help me to enjoy the abundance You've given me with the proper perspective, that these things don't bring the deep and lasting fulfillment I can only get from You. Guide my thoughts and actions to be motivated by eternal value rather than worldly gain. I surrender my life to You and rest in the loving care I know You have for me. In Your sweet name, I pray. Amen.*

Psalm 40

In tonight's psalm, King David pleads for help from God, while also thanking Him for the many things He has already done on David's behalf. Thanking God fuels our faith and reminds us that He will continue to help us now just as He has done in our past. Our pleas can then be laced with hope, knowing that He is our help and comfort.

As you prepare for tonight's meditation, inhale the blessing of God's presence in your life, and exhale your worries into His hands. Remember the good He has done in your past and take comfort in knowing He'll receive all that troubles you right now.

> I waited patiently for the LORD.
> > He turned to me and heard my cry.
> He lifted me out of the pit of destruction,
> > out of the sticky mud.
> He stood me on a rock
> > and made my feet steady.
> He put a new song in my mouth,
> > a song of praise to our God. . . .
> LORD my God, You have done many miracles.
> > Your plans for us are many.
> If I tried to tell them all,
> > there would be too many to count. . . .
> LORD, do not hold back Your mercy from me;
> > let Your love and truth always protect me.
> Troubles have surrounded me;
> > there are too many to count.
> My sins have caught me
> > so that I cannot see a way to escape. . . .
> People are trying to kill me. . . .
> > People want to hurt me. . . .
> People are making fun of me.
> > Let them be shamed into silence.
> But let those who follow You
> > be happy and glad. . . .
> LORD, because I am poor and helpless,
> > please remember me.

You are my helper and savior.
My God, do not wait.

PSALM 40:1-3, 5, 11-12, 14-17 NCV

ADORATION: In His Word, God reminds us of our great need for Him. We need not worry about His foundation shaking or crumbling; the same hands that built the foundation of the world are the hands that give us a firm foundation in our lives. You can praise His name as you rest tonight, knowing He will help you—you are safe and secure in His strong, loving hands.

CONFESSION: Think of a time when you allowed your worries and anxiety to distract you from God's faithfulness to you. Ask for His forgiveness and for relief from those fears. Ask for His help to keep your eyes on Him, even when you are struggling while waiting for your prayers to be answered.

THANKSGIVING: Thank God for the wonderful things He has done in your life. Thank Him for the prayers He has answered faithfully in your past as well as the ones He will answer on your behalf in the future.

SUPPLICATION: *Father, I love You and thank You for the many ways You've delivered me through trials. You have been so faithful to meet my needs and provide hope that has helped my heart remain inspired and steadfast. I release to You now my requests for help and peace, and I trust that You will lead me on safe ground. Hold me through this night and give me deep, peaceful rest to refresh and restore my tired body. My praise for You will ever be on my lips. Amen.*

Psalm 41

The Bible assures us that we will never have to face difficulties alone. God always meets us and helps us in our distress. His grace covers us as we rest assured that He is always by our side, comforting us and protecting us through the long nights.

Take a moment now to wind down from the day and release the worries on your mind. Bring your thoughts, your worries, and your fears to the Lord, asking Him to lift your burden. Allow yourself to trust completely in Him to carry your burdens and bless you with His peace.

Blessed are those who have regard for the weak;
the Lord delivers them in times of trouble.
The Lord protects and preserves them—
they are counted among the blessed in the land—
He does not give them over to the desire of their foes.
The Lord sustains them on their sickbed
and restores them from their bed of illness.
I said, "Have mercy on me, Lord;
heal me, for I have sinned against You."
My enemies say of me in malice,
"When will he die and his name perish?"
When one of them comes to see me,
he speaks falsely, while his heart gathers slander;
then he goes out and spreads it around.
All my enemies whisper together against me;
they imagine the worst for me, saying,
"A vile disease has afflicted him;
he will never get up from the place where he lies."
Even my close friend,
someone I trusted,
one who shared my bread,
has turned against me.
But may You have mercy on me, Lord;
raise me up, that I may repay them.
I know that You are pleased with me,
for my enemy does not triumph over me.

Because of my integrity You uphold me
and set me in Your presence forever.
Praise be to the LORD, the God of Israel,
from everlasting to everlasting.
Amen and Amen.

PSALM 41

ADORATION: God's Word reminds us He never leaves us. He never abandons us. He walks with us in our greatest trials, and He gives us strength in our weakest moments. When all seems lost, He reminds us nothing is ever lost with Him. In His power, He can heal us. In His peace, He can comfort us. In His strength, we can rest securely and safely through the night. Worship Him now for His love and kindness to you. Open your heart and be glad.

CONFESSION: Think of a time when you've been under trial and you labored in your own logic and strength rather than relying on God to bring you to victory. Ask God to forgive you and allow His grace and love to wash over you.

THANKSGIVING: Think of a time when you experienced God's deliverance, His healing, His loving presence. Praise Him for the miracles He has done; for protecting you and sustaining you through difficult times.

SUPPLICATION: *Father, I cry out to You tonight with all that weighs on my heart. I admit I cannot face my trials alone—I need Your help, Your strength, Your deliverance. May I feel your presence and comfort with me tonight. I relinquish myself into Your care through this night and into tomorrow. In Jesus' name, I pray. Amen.*

Psalm 42

In life we all face times when our heart is downcast, and we wonder how God is working in our circumstances. We want Him to take away our distress, yet He seems so far away. Does this mean that He is? No—His Word says He will never leave us nor forsake us. The question then is, will we praise Him anyway? Yes, let us long for Him as the psalmist did, as a deer longs for streams of water—living water for the soul. In our longing, His hope can fill our hearts and sustain us through difficult times.

Tonight, as you step into the quiet and calm of your surroundings, let yourself relax and surrender to the caring arms of Christ. Believe and know that God is with you. He hears your prayers and is close to your heart.

As the deer pants for streams of water,
* so my soul pants for You, my God.*
My soul thirsts for God, for the living God.
* When can I go and meet with God?*
My tears have been my food
* day and night,*
while people say to me all day long,
* "Where is your God?"*
These things I remember
* as I pour out my soul:*
how I used to go to the house of God
* under the protection of the Mighty One*
with shouts of joy and praise
* among the festive throng. . . .*
Deep calls to deep
* in the roar of Your waterfalls;*
all Your waves and breakers
* have swept over me.*
By day the Lord *directs His love,*
* at night His song is with me—*
* a prayer to the God of my life.*
I say to God my Rock,
* "Why have You forgotten me?*

Why must I go about mourning,
    oppressed by the enemy?"
My bones suffer mortal agony
    as my foes taunt me,
saying to me all day long,
    "Where is your God?"
Why, my soul, are you downcast?
    Why so disturbed within me?
Put your hope in God,
    for I will yet praise Him,
    my Savior and my God.

PSALM 42:1-4, 7-11

ADORATION: Like a deer pants for water, your soul pants for God and can only be quenched by His eternal springs of life. Allow Him to cleanse you now and satisfy you as you lay your head down to rest, bringing you refreshment. Close your eyes as you worship Him for who He is.

CONFESSION: Think of a difficult time when you lost hope in God, remembering how He brought you through. Ask for His forgiveness in your doubt and ask Him to remind you of all the good things He has done in your life.

THANKSGIVING: Praise God for His faithfulness. Praise Him for the times He has delivered you and comforted you. Praise Him for refreshing your spirit and satisfying your soul with His love and His presence that never leaves you.

SUPPLICATION: *Dear Lord, when I feel hopeless, may I feel Your calming presence and be refreshed and renewed by You. Help me to believe in Your truth, that You are with me and that You care about the little and the big things in my life. May Your presence fill my room and linger as I sleep. I want to rest in Your love and protection for sweet, refreshing sleep. I praise You and give You glory. Amen.*

Psalm 43

We live in a broken world. We see wars among the nations, strife in our communities, and even dissension in our churches. Our personal journeys are filled with trials and challenges at times. Where is God in it all? As the Bible tells us, He is our light of truth, leading us through the brokenness with hope. He is our refuge to take shelter in. He is our strength.

God's light and truth are a constant guide during difficult times. In the darkness and uncertainty of this night, ask God to guide you now to a place where you can dwell safely in Him and release your worries into His care.

> Vindicate me, my God,
>   and plead my cause
>   against an unfaithful nation.
> Rescue me from those who are
>   deceitful and wicked.
> You are God my stronghold.
>   Why have You rejected me?
> Why must I go about mourning,
>   oppressed by the enemy?
> Send me Your light and Your faithful care,
>   let them lead me;
> let them bring me to Your holy mountain,
>   to the place where You dwell.
> Then I will go to the altar of God,
>   to God, my joy and my delight.
> I will praise You with the lyre,
>   O God, my God.
> Why, my soul, are you downcast?
>   Why so disturbed within me?
> Put your hope in God,
>   for I will yet praise Him,
>   my Savior and my God.

PSALM 43

ADORATION: John 8:12 describes Jesus as the light of the world. In the darkness of the night, He will faithfully guide you with His light to a safe, secure place where your mind, body, and soul can rest. Lift up your concerns to Him and allow His truth to lighten your heart and bring comfort to your soul.

CONFESSION: Confess any fears and worries that are keeping you up tonight, giving them over to God. Ask Him to forgive you for not trusting in Him more. Receive His mercy and grace as you completely surrender to Him and put your trust in Him tonight.

THANKSGIVING: Praise God for His strength. Thank Him for the times He has been faithful to you in your life. Thank Him for the times He has sustained you through difficult moments.

SUPPLICATION: *Father, I pray now over the worries I hold on to and the lack of faith I allow into my heart. Please soothe my soul and take my anxieties. Help me to find rest in Your care. Be my refuge, my strong tower on which I can stand and remain safe. In Jesus' name, I lift up this prayer. Amen.*

Psalm 44

Tonight's psalm begins with a story about how God's mighty hand drove out the wicked nations and gave His people a place to rest safely in their land. Those same hands that protected His people back then will deliver you from the fears and worries that attack your mind tonight. At times it may seem as though He isn't working on your behalf, but He is—constantly. The important thing is not to lose heart and to remain strong in your faith in Him.

Surrender to Him now and trust that, in His arms, you can rest securely through the night. He is strong enough and caring enough to take your burdens from the day and protect you through the night. Focus your thoughts now on His faithfulness in your life and be confident that He is with you as you sleep.

O God, we have heard of the glorious miracles You did in the days of long ago. Our forefathers have told us how You drove the heathen nations from this land and gave it all to us, . . . They did not conquer by their own strength and skill, but by Your mighty power. . . .

You are my King and my God. Decree victories for Your people. For it is only by Your power and through Your name that we tread down our enemies; I do not trust my weapons. They could never save me. Only You can give us the victory over those who hate us. . . .

And yet for a time, O Lord, You have tossed us aside in dishonor and have not helped us in our battles. . . . The neighboring nations mock and laugh at us because of all the evil You have sent. . . . I am constantly despised, mocked, taunted, and cursed by my vengeful enemies. . . .

For we are facing death threats constantly because of serving You! . . . Waken! Rouse yourself! Don't sleep, O Lord! . . . Why do You look the other way? Why do You ignore our sorrows and oppression? We lie face downward in the dust. Rise up, O Lord, and come and help us. Save us by Your constant love.

PSALM 44:1, 3-7, 9, 13, 15-16, 22-26 TLB

ADORATION: Think about the Lord as your King. What does this mean to you? Allow His power and care to bring you hope and comfort. Close your eyes and imagine God leading the way through your trials and tribulations. Imagine His hands striking anything that stands against you. Worship Him for His faithfulness to you in the past as well as in your current circumstances.

CONFESSION: Think of a time when you put your hope in something or someone else other than the Lord. Confess any idols you are depending on and ask for His forgiveness. Ask Him to help you put your hope and trust in Him above all else.

THANKSGIVING: Rejoice in His name. Thank Him for the times He has rescued you and helped you. Thank Him in advance for the future troubles He will deliver you from.

SUPPLICATION: *Lord, I want to release my troubles to You now and rest in Your arms tonight. I believe You are for me and that You will deliver me from the pressures I face. I cast my fears and anxiety onto You and trust that You are working toward the victory You have in store for me. In Jesus' name, I pray. Amen.*

Psalm 45

The Bible uses the metaphor of marriage to depict Christ's relationship with the Church. Throughout Scripture, Christ is referred to as the bridegroom, and the Church is referred to as the bride of Christ. This psalm is a beautiful poem describing a royal wedding that perfectly illustrates our future with Christ. In the same way a bride spends time preparing herself for her prince, our lives are a period of preparation for the day we will meet our King.

Imagine what rejoicing there will be in a holy union with Him. Picture Him as the majestic Crown of all, ruling in truth, humility, and justice—and One who is completely devoted to protecting you and sustaining you through the night. Allow your hope in the Lord to take hold of and renew your spirit.

> My heart is stirred by a noble theme
>> as I recite my verses for the king;
>> my tongue is the pen of a skillful writer.
> You are the most excellent of men
>> and Your lips have been anointed with grace,
>> since God has blessed You forever.
> Gird Your sword on Your side, You Mighty One;
>> clothe Yourself with splendor and majesty.
> In Your majesty ride forth victoriously
>> in the cause of truth, humility and justice;
>> let Your right hand achieve awesome deeds. . . .
> Your throne, O God, will last for ever and ever;
>> a scepter of justice will be the scepter of Your kingdom. . . .
> All Your robes are fragrant with myrrh and aloes and cassia;
>> from palaces adorned with ivory
>> the music of the strings makes You glad.
> Daughters of kings are among Your honored women;
>> at Your right hand is the royal bride in gold of Ophir. . . .
> All glorious is the princess within her chamber;
>> her gown is interwoven with gold.
> In embroidered garments she is led to the king;
>> her virgin companions follow her—

those brought to be with her.
Led in with joy and gladness,
    they enter the palace of the King.
Your sons will take the place of Your fathers;
    You will make them princes throughout the land.
I will perpetuate Your memory through all generations;
    therefore the nations will praise You for ever and ever.

PSALM 45: 1-4, 6, 8-9, 13-17

ADORATION: Praise God for the joy and gladness you have in your heart as you think about approaching the noble throne of the almighty King. Give all praise and worship to Him as you remember that He will reign forever and ever.

CONFESSION: Think of a time when you took God's greatness for granted. Ask for His forgiveness and His help with focusing on a bright and amazing future with Him.

THANKSGIVING: Rejoice in the Lord by thanking Him for the plans He has for you. Praise Him for His care as your King.

SUPPLICATION: *Father, thank You for all that You've set into place so that I can have a glorious eternal future with You. Help my focus, my deeds, my actions, and my thoughts be ever mindful of You and the sacrifice You made on my behalf. Draw my heart toward Your presence and Your holiness—as though every day is a wedding day with You. All glory and honor to You. Amen.*

Psalm 46

The world can feel like a scary place sometimes, but God's Word tells us not to be afraid. We have help and a refuge in which to dwell, the Lord's loving arms. He is bigger than any problem we face, and He's the answer to the hope we hold on to.

Step into the safe haven of God, whose strength and power will protect you; be still and know that He will protect you through this night and into a new day.

> God is our refuge and strength,
>   an ever-present help in trouble.
> Therefore we will not fear, though the earth give way
>   and the mountains fall into the heart of the sea,
> though its waters roar and foam
>   and the mountains quake with their surging. . . .
> Nations are in uproar, kingdoms fall;
>   He lifts His voice, the earth melts.
> The LORD Almighty is with us;
>   the God of Jacob is our fortress. . . .
> He makes wars cease
>   to the ends of the earth.
> He breaks the bow and shatters the spear;
>   He burns the shields with fire.
> He says, "Be still, and know that I am God;
>   I will be exalted among the nations,
>   I will be exalted in the earth."
> The LORD Almighty is with us;
>   the God of Jacob is our fortress.

PSALM 46:1–3, 6–7, 9–11

ADORATION: This passage describes God as our fortress, our refuge and strength, our ever-present help in trouble. It is clear God is always there to help us, to keep us secure, and to bring us peace. As you lie down to go to sleep, you have nothing to fear because God's plan has always been to rescue you, from the very beginning of time. Thank Him that He is always there to help you, to keep you secure, and to be your peace. As you wind down to sleep, surrender any fear you're holding on to and trust in His presence over you tonight.

CONFESSION: Think of a time when you were overcome by fear and you didn't go to God as your refuge. Confess this situation to Him now and allow Him to take away your fears and give you His peace.

THANKSGIVING: Rejoice in the Lord's strength. Praise Him for the times He has helped you and delivered you. Thank Him for rescuing you; thank Him for keeping you safe and secure tonight.

SUPPLICATION: *Father, I look to You now and release my fears and insecurities into Your hands. Be my refuge and strength tonight; deliver me from my difficult circumstances. Fill me with Your peace and give me deep, sound sleep through this night that only You can give. In Jesus' name, I pray. Amen.*

Psalm 47

No matter what is happening in our lives or in our world, we can always find joy and hope in the power and sovereignty of the Lord. Praising God for who He is, rather than for what He does, changes our perspective and allows us to experience all the wonderful things God has for us—His joy, hope, and peace.

As you wind down from the day, turn your focus to this truth, acknowledging that God is the all-powerful. Rest assured that He is in control over all the events in your world and all the circumstances in your life. As your King, He cares about your life and works for your good, for you are His, and He is your God.

Now surrender to the almighty King and ask Him to speak to you through tonight's psalm. Allow the truth of who He is to bring you comfort and hope as you sleep.

> *Clap your hands, all you nations;*
> *shout to God with cries of joy.*
> *For the LORD Most High is awesome,*
> *the great King over all the earth.*
> *He subdued nations under us,*
> *peoples under our feet.*
> *He chose our inheritance for us,*
> *the pride of Jacob, whom He loved.*
> *God has ascended amid shouts of joy,*
> *the LORD amid the sounding of trumpets.*
> *Sing praises to God, sing praises;*
> *sing praises to our King, sing praises.*
> *For God is the King of all the earth;*
> *sing to Him a psalm of praise.*
> *God reigns over the nations;*
> *God is seated on His holy throne.*
> *The nobles of the nations assemble*
> *as the people of the God of Abraham,*
> *for the kings of the earth belong to God;*
> *He is greatly exalted.*

PSALM 47

ADORATION: Close your eyes and imagine God as the powerful, almighty King sitting on His heavenly throne, where He rules the nations and watches over His people. This same King that has the power to create and destroy nations is the King who knows every detail about you and uses His power to protect you and preserve you. Praise Him for the glorious King He is!

CONFESSION: Think of a time when you lost sight of God, trusting in worldly things rather than in God. Ask for His forgiveness. Pray He will help you keep your eyes on Him and turn your ears toward His Word as you navigate this world.

THANKSGIVING: Praise the Lord for His power and sovereignty. Thank Him for being the One you can count on and turn to for everything. Thank Him for the wonderful inheritance that awaits you as a child of the one, true King.

SUPPLICATION: *Lord, I'm both grateful and relieved to know that You are sovereign and in absolute control. Help me not to lean on my own, but to trust in You and Your almighty power. I pray for the leaders of this nation, that they would unite and be of one mind toward You. Give them discernment and courage to do the work before them. All glory and honor to You. Amen.*

Psalm 48

The whole earth is His, and it blesses Him! As you transition from the day into the evening, may you gain inspiration from the way the earth turns to God in worship, love, and praise. Clear your mind and release your fears, worries, and doubts to God.

Lie still and imagine a beautiful city filled with the glory of the Lord, fortified with His strength. Like this beautiful city, the Lord is within you, protecting you and sustaining you; He is your fortress. Ask Him to inscribe His Word on your heart so that you can carry His truth and love with you into the night. You can rest knowing He is watching over you throughout the night.

The LORD is great and highly praised
in the city of our God.
His holy mountain, rising splendidly,
is the joy of the whole earth.
Mount Zion—the summit of Zaphon—
is the city of the great King.
God is known as a stronghold
in its citadels. . . .
God, within Your temple,
we contemplate Your faithful love.
Like Your name, God, so Your praise
reaches to the ends of the earth;
Your right hand is filled with justice.
Mount Zion is glad.
Judah's villages rejoice
because of Your judgments.
Go around Zion, encircle it;
count its towers,
note its ramparts; tour its citadels
so that you can tell a future generation:
"This God, our God forever and ever—
He will always lead us."

PSALM 48:1-3, 9-14 CSB

ADORATION: Rest in His presence, knowing you are safe and secure in Him. Rejoice in His righteousness. Know His Word will never die, and His love will never fail. Thank Him for who He is.

CONFESSION: Think of a time when your complaints and doubt toward God outnumbered your praise. Confess this to Him now and ask Him to continually remind you of who He is and who you are to Him—beloved.

THANKSGIVING: Praise the Lord for His strength and power. Praise Him for the times He has protected you and the love He has for you.

SUPPLICATION: *Father, I look to You now and praise You from deep within my heart—Your goodness is too great to fathom. Create in me a daily habit of reading Your Word. May I turn to You for guidance, protection, discernment, and truth. Help me to rest in Your perfect peace tonight as I remember and dwell on Your faithfulness to me. In Jesus' name, I pray. Amen.*

Psalm 49

The Bible reminds us that riches on earth are temporary, but the riches we store in heaven are eternal (see Matthew 6:19–21). But what does this mean? As you prepare for your quiet time with God, look around at all the possessions you hold dear. Now try to imagine how these pale in comparison to the eternal treasures waiting for you in heaven, where you will be face-to-face with God.

Tonight, put your hope and trust in the things of God rather than in the things of this world.

My mouth speaks wisdom;
my heart's meditation brings understanding.
I turn my ear to a proverb;
I explain my riddle with a lyre.
Why should I fear in times of trouble?
The iniquity of my foes surrounds me.
They trust in their wealth
and boast of their abundant riches.
Yet these cannot redeem a person
or pay his ransom to God. . . .
For one can see that the wise die;
the foolish and stupid also pass away.
Then they leave their wealth to others.
Their graves are their permanent homes,
their dwellings from generation to generation,
though they have named estates after themselves.
But despite his assets, mankind will not last;
he is like the animals that perish.
This is the way of those who are arrogant,
and of their followers,
who approve of their words. Selah. . . .
Do not be afraid when a person gets rich,
when the wealth of his house increases.
For when he dies, he will take nothing at all;
his wealth will not follow him down.
Though he blesses himself during his lifetime—

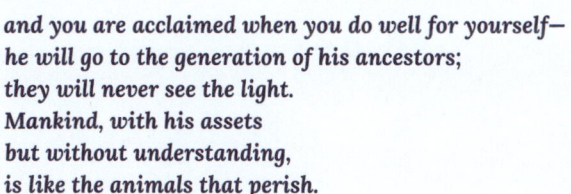

and you are acclaimed when you do well for yourself—
he will go to the generation of his ancestors;
they will never see the light.
Mankind, with his assets
but without understanding,
is like the animals that perish.

PSALM 49:3-7, 10-13, 16-20 CSB

ADORATION: In our world, many wealthy people are praised and exalted because of their personal accomplishments and worldly success. But the Bible warns us not to put value in worldly treasures. The psalmist beautifully reminds us that we will all face death and decay, but those who put their trust in the Lord will be redeemed and restored for eternity. What a gift! As you put your hope and trust in the Lord, exalt Him for the bright future you have with Him.

CONFESSION: Think of a time when you put too much value in material possessions and worldly wealth. Confess any times when you served money over God. Ask for His forgiveness and ask for His help in guarding your heart and mind from the temptations of this world.

THANKSGIVING: Praise the Lord for the way God has provided for you. Take a moment to thank Him for the material ways He has blessed you, while remembering that your possessions are secondary to the contentment and joy you can find in Him.

SUPPLICATION: *Lord, help me to keep money and material possessions secondary to You. Please deliver me from the temptation to focus on and serve my possessions rather than You. Help me to be content and generous with what You provide and to focus on building heavenly treasures rather than earthly wealth. Thank You for Your promise of an eternal home with You! In Jesus' name. Amen.*

Psalm 50

When someone gives us a gift, it's only natural to express our gratitude for their kindness and thoughtfulness. So as each day draws to a close, we have the opportunity to slow down, look around, and reflect on all that God has given us. No matter what type of day you've had, there is reason for rejoicing. He says, "For the world and everything in it is Mine" (Psalm 50:12 CSB). This includes you and the blessings He's provided for your life.

Take a deep breath and release the trials of the day. Praise Him for His gifts and for His justice. Praising God is pleasing to Him and helps us to listen for His tender whispers of love in return. Tonight, let's commit ourselves to the Lord as we experience His hope and peace as we lie down to rest.

> The Mighty One, God, the LORD,
>   speaks and summons the earth
>   from the rising of the sun to where it sets.
> From Zion, perfect in beauty,
>   God shines forth. . . .
> He summons the heavens above,
>   and the earth, that He may judge His people:
> "Gather to Me this consecrated people,
>   who made a covenant with Me by sacrifice."
> And the heavens proclaim His righteousness,
>   for He is a God of justice.
> "Listen, My people, and I will speak; . . .
> I have no need of a bull from your stall
>   or of goats from your pens,
> for every animal of the forest is Mine,
>   and the cattle on a thousand hills.
> I know every bird in the mountains,
>   and the insects in the fields are mine.
> If I were hungry I would not tell you,
>   for the world is Mine, and all that is in it. . . .
> Sacrifice thank offerings to God,
>   fulfill your vows to the Most High,

and call on Me in the day of trouble;
I will deliver you, and you will honor Me." . . .
"Those who sacrifice thank offerings honor Me,
and to the blameless I will show My salvation."

PSALM 50:1-2, 4-7, 9-12, 14-15, 23

ADORATION: This psalm talks about honoring God with an offering. As you think about the ways God has worked in your life, can you offer your life to Him once more? Lay down your life at His feet and find rest in your commitment to the Lord.

CONFESSION: Acknowledge any unconfessed sin before the Lord and ask for His forgiveness. Ask Him to help you love Him and obey Him. Ask Him to teach you what it means to follow Him.

THANKSGIVING: Praise the Lord for His righteousness, for His mercy and justice. Praise Him for His love and forgiveness. Thank Him for the blessings He has given you and for the times He has helped you and delivered you.

SUPPLICATION: *Father, thank You for Your presence, Your creation, Your loving-kindness, and Your provision. All that I have is Yours; may I always remember this. I am grateful for Your joy and peace—may they fill my heart and cover me through this night. In Jesus' name. Amen.*

Psalm 51

God's Word tells us that nothing can separate us from His love (see Romans 8:31–39). But if we allow unconfessed sin in our lives to remain, our relationship with God is hindered. He can seem far away when, in reality, He longs to be near to us as we confess our sins and ask for His forgiveness.

Psalm 51 is a beautiful liturgy of King David's heartfelt plea after he committed a sin, and it's a great example of the heartfelt outpouring of honesty God wants from us. When our conscience is weighed down with something we know we shouldn't have done, He wants us to come and release it to Him. It is God's desire not to condemn us, but to cleanse and restore us to Himself. And when this happens, we are able to completely rest in His arms, free from burdens and able to soak in His unfailing love.

Tonight, as you let go of the trials of the day, bring the heaviest pieces of your heart to God and receive healing and freedom in His forgiveness.

> Be gracious to me, God,
> according to Your faithful love;
> according to Your abundant compassion,
> blot out my rebellion.
> Completely wash away my guilt
> and cleanse me from my sin.
> For I am conscious of my rebellion,
> and my sin is always before me.
> Against You—You alone—I have sinned
> and done this evil in Your sight. . . .
> Surely You desire integrity in the inner self,
> and You teach me wisdom deep within.
> Purify me with hyssop, and I will be clean;
> wash me, and I will be whiter than snow.
> Let me hear joy and gladness;
> let the bones you have crushed rejoice. . . .
> God, create a clean heart for me
> and renew a steadfast spirit within me.
> Do not banish me from your presence

or take Your Holy Spirit from me.
Restore the joy of Your salvation to me,
and sustain me by giving me a willing spirit. . . .
The sacrifice pleasing to God is a broken spirit.
You will not despise a broken and humbled heart, God.

PSALM 51:1-4, 6-8, 10-12, 17 CSB

ADORATION: At night, when we're in a quiet, dark place, we sometimes struggle with our sin and shame, making it hard to find rest. But God wants us to bring our heaviness to Him so that He can cleanse us and free us. Thank Him now for His mercy, grace, and restoration that our mind, body, and soul so desperately need.

CONFESSION: Confess any sin to the Lord and ask for His forgiveness. Ask Him to help you face any consequences of your sin and to restore the joy of your relationship with Him.

THANKSGIVING: Praise the Lord for His righteousness. Thank Him for the grace and love He has shown you and will show you tonight.

SUPPLICATION: *Lord, I humble myself tonight and acknowledge my sin. Forgive me now and deliver me from temptation that the evil one brings. Create in me a pure heart and renew my spirit as I rest in You tonight. Thank You for Your grace and love and the supernatural peace You give. In Your great name, I pray. Amen.*

Psalm 52

Our world can make us fearful of this present time and worried about our future. We can't stop bad things from occurring and bad people from prospering, but we can control our response. When evil does occur, He does not allow it to prosper forever—His justice will prevail. While we wait on His justice, we can safely remain in His care. He sees all things and will be a refuge as we claim His promise not only to protect us, but to help us *flourish* (see Psalm 52:8 CSB). He loves those who are faithful to Him, so tonight, let's put our confidence in Him and find rest knowing we are safe and secure in His hands.

> *Why boast about evil, you hero!*
> *God's faithful love is constant....*
> *You love evil instead of good,*
> *lying instead of speaking truthfully. Selah*
> *You love any words that destroy,*
> *you treacherous tongue! ...*
> *The righteous will see and fear,*
> *and they will derisively say about that hero,*
> *"Here is the man*
> *who would not make God his refuge,*
> *but trusted in the abundance of his riches,*
> *taking refuge in his destructive behavior."*
> *But I am like a flourishing olive tree*
> *in the house of God;*
> *I trust in God's faithful love forever and ever.*
> *I will praise You forever for what You have done.*
> *In the presence of Your faithful people,*
> *I will put my hope in Your name, for it is good.*

PSALM 52:1, 3–4, 6–9 CSB

ADORATION: Meditating on God's Word shifts our perspective of the world around us. We are reassured that He is in control, and He is the virtuous judge who will make things right. Look to Him in adoration, finding hope and peace and rest in Him.

CONFESSION: Think of a time when you tried to bring your own form of justice to a difficult situation. Ask for God's forgiveness in this situation and for Him to help you trust Him to make things right.

THANKSGIVING: Put your hope in the name of the Lord once again. Praise Him for His goodness and for His unfailing love. Thank Him for the times His justice has prevailed in your life and in our world. Thank Him for the times He has sustained you.

SUPPLICATION: *Father, I need Your help navigating through all this world's injustices. Please sustain me through times of difficulty and persecution, strengthening me in Your name. Take my fears and replace them with Your peace; help me to sleep soundly without worry. Thank You for being with me through this night. In Jesus' name. Amen.*

Psalm 53

Tonight's psalm is a direct reminder that we are all sinners—we all fall short of the glory of God. However, there is good news even here—God chose to rescue us and redeem us through His Son rather than leave us in our sin. It is in this hope and promise that we can find comfort as we end the day and lie down to rest.

Close your eyes and imagine God looking down on the earth, trying to find those who seek Him and love Him. When He sees your heart seeking after Him, He fixes His gaze on you. And when He does, know He sees Christ in you, covering and cleansing you of your sin. He takes delight in this! Because of the covering of His Son, He will protect you and preserve you through the day and night.

> The fool says in his heart,
>   "There is no God."
> They are corrupt, and their ways are vile;
>   there is no one who does good.
> God looks down from heaven
>   on all mankind
> to see if there are any who understand,
>   any who seek God.
> Everyone has turned away, all have become corrupt;
>   there is no one who does good,
>   not even one.
> Do all these evildoers know nothing? . . .
> But there they are, overwhelmed with dread,
>   where there was nothing to dread.
> God scattered the bones of those who attacked you;
>   you put them to shame, for God despised them.
> Oh, that salvation for Israel would come out of Zion!
>   When God restores His people,
>   let Jacob rejoice and Israel be glad!

PSALM 53

ADORATION: Jesus didn't come to this earth to condemn us and leave us in our sin—He came to save us and replace our sin with His righteousness. He loves to cleanse us and remove any barrier there may be between us and Him. Praise God, adoring and thanking the One who loves us.

CONFESSION: Think of a time when you turned away from God to do what you wanted, knowing He didn't approve. Ask for His forgiveness and ask Him to help you stay on the perfect path He has for your life.

THANKSGIVING: Praise God for who He is—loving, kind, full of grace. Thank Him for redeeming you and entering into a relationship with you. Thank Him for the times when He has protected you.

SUPPLICATION: *Lord, I look to You and seek You now, asking Your forgiveness for the times I've strayed. I want to be close to You and follow the path You have for me. Cleanse me of my sin and protect me as I receive the supernatural peace that only You can give through this night. Help me to receive and walk in the fullness of Your grace. Watch over me now as I surrender to You as I sleep. All praise and glory to You. Amen.*

Psalm 54

God tells us we will face persecution and trouble in this world, but today's psalm reminds us to look to God to deliver us from those who rise against us. We shouldn't be afraid because there is nothing God can't help us overcome. When we face trouble, we are to look to Him for His strength and for His help.

As you lie down to rest, set down your troubles at His feet and allow Him to take up the fight for you. As you recall your hurts from the day, take a deep breath and imagine God's strength filling your chest. Now exhale slowly and imagine His healing power restoring you. Seek to find comfort as you meditate on His Word tonight.

> Save me, O God, by Your name;
>   vindicate me by Your might.
> Hear my prayer, O God;
>   listen to the words of my mouth.
> Arrogant foes are attacking me;
>   ruthless people are trying to kill me—
>   people without regard for God.
> Surely God is my help;
>   the Lord is the one who sustains me.
> Let evil recoil on those who slander me;
>   in Your faithfulness destroy them.
> I will sacrifice a freewill offering to You;
>   I will praise Your name, LORD, for it is good.
> You have delivered me from all my troubles,
>   and my eyes have looked in triumph on my foes.
>
> **PSALM 54**

ADORATION: God promises to deliver us through our trials, and that includes the pain we feel that others have inflicted. He will protect us from those who rise against us. He is a God of love, who cares without fail. Worship Him now for loving you.

CONFESSION: Think of a time when you took revenge upon someone who had wronged you. Confess any bitterness and resentment you may still harbor in your heart. Ask God for His forgiveness. Ask Him to help you trust Him to deliver you from those who are against you.

THANKSGIVING: Praise the name of the Lord, for He is good. Praise Him for His faithfulness. Thank Him for the times when He has helped you and delivered you from trouble.

SUPPLICATION: *Lord, I want Your Word to soak into my soul and bring the comfort I need right now. Give me Your strength to remain steadfast no matter what I face and deliver me from all the circumstances that trouble me. Remove the anxiety within my heart and replace it with Your presence as I sleep. I love You and look to You for the rest I long for. In Jesus' name. Amen.*

Psalm 55

When we face opposition from those around us or when we have been betrayed by a loved one, we might want to leave everyone and everything behind to escape our painful reality. But the Bible tells us we don't have to flee. Rather than running away, we should run to God and quiet our minds and hearts in prayer and worship to find relief from our pain and hurt. With God by our side, we can face our troubles with His strength, lift our burdens to find peace, and call on His name to find hope.

Tonight, let's find strength and solace in God's Word and in His presence.

Listen to my prayer, O God,
    do not ignore my plea;
    hear me and answer me.
My thoughts trouble me and I am distraught
    because of what my enemy is saying,
    because of the threats of the wicked; . . .
My heart is in anguish within me; . . .
Fear and trembling have beset me; . . .
I said, "Oh, that I had the wings of a dove!
    I would fly away and be at rest. . . .
If an enemy were insulting me,
    I could endure it;
if a foe were rising against me,
    I could hide.
But it is you, a man like myself,
    my companion, my close friend,
    with whom I once enjoyed sweet fellowship. . . .
As for me, I call to God,
    and the Lord saves me.
Evening, morning and noon
    I cry out in distress,
    and He hears my voice.
He rescues me unharmed
    from the battle waged against me,
    even though many oppose me. . . .
Cast your cares on the Lord

and He will sustain you;
He will never let
    the righteous be shaken.
But You, God, will bring down the wicked
    into the pit of decay; . . .
But as for me, I trust in You.

PSALM 55:1-6, 12-14, 16-18, 22-23

ADORATION: Take a few moments to meditate on the goodness and faithfulness of God. Know He is the One who never changes; you can always count on His promise to see you, to know your hurt, to love you, and to sustain you through it. Visualize God restoring and redeeming whatever has been broken in your life. Receive His warm embrace and worship Him for His loving-kindness to you.

CONFESSION: Think of a time when a close friend or a family member betrayed you. Confess any unforgiveness, anger, or bitterness that is still in your heart to God. Ask God to help you forgive others the way He forgives you.

THANKSGIVING: Praise God for His goodness and faithfulness. Thank Him for never changing and for being the One you can always count on. Thank Him for sustaining you every day and night.

SUPPLICATION: *Lord, I turn to You now for help with putting the pieces of my broken heart back together. I confess I think about ways to hurt others in return rather than seek to repair. Help me to lean into You for the strength I need to forgive them the way You forgive me. Heal my heart and help me to remember that You are with me in this moment and I can rest in Your care. With a grateful heart, I pray. Amen.*

Psalm 56

In the darkness and stillness of the night, our fears, hurts, and worries can linger and keep us from experiencing the peace and restful sleep we long for. Yet there is great comfort in knowing that God not only sees our troubles, but He also puts our tears into His bottle of care. When we are afraid, we can trust in Him with our whole heart. When we cry out to Him, we can know with full conviction that He is for us.

Tonight, join in the psalmist's prayer to put your trust in God and allow His presence to help you find rest. As your mind calms, meditate on God's promises. Think about the bright future He has for you. There is nothing that can defeat you, not even death. He has already delivered you and saved you. Let His joy fill your heart as you contemplate what He has done for you.

> Be merciful to me, my God,
>   for my enemies are in hot pursuit;
>   all day long they press their attack. . . .
> When I am afraid, I put my trust in You.
>   In God, whose word I praise—
> in God I trust and am not afraid.
>   What can mere mortals do to me?
> All day long they twist my words;
>   all their schemes are for my ruin.
> They conspire, they lurk,
>   they watch my steps,
>   hoping to take my life. . . .
> Record my misery;
>   list my tears on Your scroll—
>   are they not in Your record?
> Then my enemies will turn back
>   when I call for help.
>   By this I will know that God is for me.
> In God, whose word I praise,
>   in the LORD, whose word I praise—
> in God I trust and am not afraid.
>   What can man do to me?

I am under vows to You, my God;
I will present my thank offerings to You.
For You have delivered me from death
and my feet from stumbling,
that I may walk before God
in the light of life.

PSALM 56:1, 3-6, 8-13

ADORATION: The Bible reminds us that God is for us, so we should not fear anyone or anything. Since He has already delivered us from death, we can put our trust in Him and be confident in His Word. Let's throw off everything that hinders us from experiencing the calming presence of the Lord and worship Him with a glad heart.

CONFESSION: Think of a time when you lost your faith and hope in God. Confess when you have allowed your fears and lack of trust to hinder your relationship with Him. Pray for God to restore the joy in your relationship with Him.

THANKSGIVING: Thank God for giving you His Word and the anchor it is for your life. Thank Him for always keeping His promises. Thank Him for the times He has delivered you.

SUPPLICATION: *Father, sometimes the fear and worry in my heart seems bigger than You, but I know they're not. Help me to trust in You more and remain firm in my faith that You are with me and that You care. Watch over me tonight and soothe my soul. Help me to find peaceful rest in the comfort and protection of Your loving arms. In Jesus' name. Amen.*

Psalm 57

When the stress and anxiety of our day is keeping us up at night, the Bible tells us we can find relief when we turn to God and His truth. When we trust in Him—fixing our heart, soul, and mind on Him—we can have full confidence in Him to help and to save us the same way the psalmist entrusted his life into God's hands when he was in danger.

As we clear our minds and release the burdens of the day, let us take heart and have that same courage. Let us have the same reliance on the One who is in control and who promises to be a refuge as the psalmist did. Let's invite God's presence into our hearts now and allow His Spirit to quiet our minds tonight and to give us strength for tomorrow.

Have mercy on me, my God, have mercy on me,
for in You I take refuge.
I will take refuge in the shadow of Your wings
until the disaster has passed.
I cry out to God Most High,
to God, who vindicates me.
He sends from heaven and saves me,
rebuking those who hotly pursue me—
God sends forth His love and His faithfulness.
I am in the midst of lions;
I am forced to dwell among ravenous beasts—
men whose teeth are spears and arrows,
whose tongues are sharp swords.
Be exalted, O God, above the heavens;
let Your glory be over all the earth.
They spread a net for my feet—
I was bowed down in distress.
They dug a pit in my path—
but they have fallen into it themselves.
My heart, O God, is steadfast,
my heart is steadfast;
I will sing and make music.

Awake, my soul!
Awake, harp and lyre!
I will awaken the dawn.
I will praise You, Lord, among the nations;
I will sing of You among the peoples.
For great is Your love, reaching to the heavens;
Your faithfulness reaches to the skies.
Be exalted, O God, above the heavens;
let Your glory be over all the earth.

PSALM 57

ADORATION: God's Word says that His faithfulness to and love for you are so great that they reach beyond the skies to the heavens. Know He wants to lift your burdens and carry them tonight to a faraway place where they will no longer weigh you down. Thank Him for His shelter, His care, and His strength for tomorrow.

CONFESSION: Think of a time when someone criticized you or slandered you and you retaliated with hateful words rather than turning to God for His help. Pray He will forgive you and help you forgive that person. Pray He will help you turn to Him when someone slanders you or criticizes you.

THANKSGIVING: Praise God for His faithfulness and love. Thank Him for the times He has protected you and delivered you.

SUPPLICATION: *Lord, when someone says or does something that hurts me, remind me that You are my peace. Give me a heart of compassion for those who lash out because of their own hurt. Help to restore what the enemy tries to break and devour. Now I ask that You fill me with Your healing love and give me rest for this night. All glory to You. Amen.*

Psalm 58

In today's psalm, David goes to God and vents all of his feelings of injustice to Him—he doesn't hold back the bad things he wishes God would do to make things right. But after he finishes, he also reminds us it is God's place to bring justice, in His way and in His time. We can derive a lot of comfort from that because David also says that those who put their trust in Him will be rewarded.

As you release the injustices you feel in your heart tonight, meditate on these words and rejoice in knowing God's justice will triumph over the evil in the world and in your life. Find freedom in knowing this justice can only be administered by God's hands. Find rest in knowing you serve the righteous Judge of the earth, and He will be with you as you sleep.

> Do you rulers indeed speak justly?
>   Do you judge people with equity?
> No, in your heart you devise injustice,
>   and your hands mete out violence on the earth. . . .
> Break the teeth in their mouths, O God;
>   LORD, tear out the fangs of those lions!
> Let them vanish like water that flows away;
>   when they draw the bow, let their arrows fall short. . . .
> Before your pots can feel the heat of the thorns—
>   whether they be green or dry—the wicked will be swept away.
> The righteous will be glad when they are avenged,
>   when they dip their feet in the blood of the wicked.
> Then people will say,
>   "Surely the righteous still are rewarded;
>   surely there is a God who judges the earth."
>
> **PSALM 58:1-2, 6-7, 9-11**

ADORATION: Tonight, remember that you may face dark days, but God's love and light will brighten your nights. Find assurance in His truth. Rest in full measure knowing He will make things right in your life and in our world, for the One who judges fairly has you in His hands.

CONFESSION: Think of a time when you were silent when you should have spoken in the face of injustice. Pray for God's forgiveness in this situation. Pray for the courage to be the voice for the vulnerable and oppressed, and pray for discernment in knowing what steps to take to stand against injustice.

THANKSGIVING: Praise God for His justice. Praise Him as the One who fairly judges every person and every situation. Thank Him for the times when He has made things right in your life.

SUPPLICATION: *Dear Lord, I pray for You to intervene in unfair situations I'm facing. Receive any thoughts of revenge I may have and replace them with the trust I need for releasing the consequences to You. Give me the patience and strength I need to wait on You. Please fill me with hope and assurance that You are with me and that I can completely rest knowing You are in control. I give You my heart to hold through this night. Amen.*

Psalm 59

We toss and turn in the night because our private concerns and deepest worries rise to the top of our thoughts, and our focus shifts to the day's struggles we've had to endure. Our energy can then turn to guarding our hearts in self-preservation, which is exhausting. But when we release our burdens to God and ask for His peace, His strength becomes our strength. His faithfulness meets us and lifts us into the stronghold of His love, and we can once again rest in His peace and His promise of continued presence.

Tonight as you wade through all your worries, turn your focus to who God is—the Almighty One who sustains you, protects you, and delivers you. Know He came to bring you rest for your mind, body, and soul. With Him in your sights, you can rest in knowing that you dwell in the safety of His arms.

Rescue me from my enemies, my God;
protect me from those who rise up against me. . . .
For no fault of mine,
they run and take up a position.
Awake to help me, and take notice. . . .
Look, they spew from their mouths—
sharp words from their lips.
"For who," they say, "will hear?" . . .
I will keep watch for You, my strength,
because God is my stronghold.
My faithful God will come to meet me;
God will let me look down on my adversaries. . . .
For the sin of their mouths and the words of their lips,
let them be caught in their pride. . . .
And they return at evening, snarling like dogs
and prowling around the city. . . .
But I will sing of Your strength
and will joyfully proclaim
Your faithful love in the morning.
For You have been a stronghold for me,
a refuge in my day of trouble.

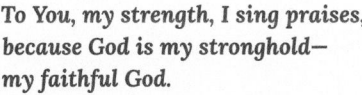

To You, my strength, I sing praises,
because God is my stronghold—
my faithful God.

PSALM 59:1, 4, 7, 9-10, 12, 14, 16-17 CSB

ADORATION: Tonight, no matter what you are facing, you can rejoice in the strength of the Lord. As you continue to wind down from the day, allow His hope to help you and save you. Visualize God striking down your fears and worries with His mighty hands. Know these same hands will hold you and preserve you through the night, giving you peace.

CONFESSION: Think of a time when you doubted God's protection and faithfulness. Pray He will help your heart, mind, and soul turn to Him in times of trouble.

THANKSGIVING: Praise God for His mercy and love, that He is a stronghold in times of trouble. Praise Him for His faithfulness. Thank Him for the strength and confidence He gives you. Thank Him for the times He has helped you.

SUPPLICATION: *Lord, please forgive me for the times I turn to my own strength when going through the battles of the day. Be my stronghold now, meet me in my trouble, and help my heart to sing once again of the faithfulness You show toward me. All praise and glory to You. Amen.*

Psalm 60

When our circumstances seem out of control, the Bible reminds us of God's power to do mighty things. And even though there are times when we feel like God doesn't hear our cries for help, His Word confirms over and over that He doesn't leave us to face the darkness in our world alone. He is here to help us and guide us through every situation we face. His power and love have no limits. Because of this, we can rest safely, knowing we are secure in God's mighty hands.

Tonight, as you close your eyes, exhale any negative thoughts that are robbing you of your joy. As you read the following psalm, know that there isn't anything you can't say to God. He wants you to be honest with Him. He hears, and He cares. Remember that, in Him, you are victorious over your fears and anxieties, including the ones you've faced today.

Now put your trust fully in God and let His Word speak to you.

> You have rejected us, God, and burst upon us;
>   You have been angry—now restore us!
> You have shaken the land and torn it open;
>   mend its fractures, for it is quaking. . . .
> But for those who fear You, You have raised a banner
>   to be unfurled against the bow.
> Save us and help us with Your right hand,
>   that those You love may be delivered. . . .
> Who will bring me to the fortified city?
>   Who will lead me to Edom?
> Is it not You, God, You who have now rejected us
>   and no longer go out with our armies?
> Give us aid against the enemy,
>   for human help is worthless.
> With God we will gain the victory,
>   and He will trample down our enemies.
>
> **PSALM 60:1-2, 4-5, 9-12**

ADORATION: Knowing God is in control can help us find freedom from our fears and worries and help us find hope and peace in the middle of chaos. He provides what we need far better than any other source. Open your heart to the love He has for you; worship Him for all He has done and will do for your life.

CONFESSION: Think on and confess any doubts you have of God's power. Ask for His forgiveness and praise Him for believing in you, even when you have not fully believed in Him. Receive His mercy and cleansing on your heart and be assured that He loves you.

THANKSGIVING: Praise God for His strength. Thank Him for the times when you have seen Him answer prayer. Thank Him for the times when He has protected you and delivered you.

SUPPLICATION: *Father, I look to You now and rely on Your deliverance of justice in this world and in my life. Please help my focus be on Your sovereignty and grace and the loving-kindness You have shown to me. I trust in You and thank You for giving me peace of mind and rest for my soul. In Jesus' name, I pray. Amen.*

Psalm 61

Wherever we are and wherever we go, God is there beside us to protect us, help us, and guide us. He wants to usher us in to a safe place in which we can find rest. We can find confirmation of this in tonight's psalm, which reveals David's heart in a time when he was without strength and needed affirmation from our Lord. We all can relate to this neediness and can find inspiration to hold on to our faith the way David did. There is hope in knowing there isn't a promise God has made that He won't keep.

He will never leave your side. He is there when you call upon Him for help—always. Tonight, as you hand over your worries to the Lord, put your confidence in Him and allow His presence to fill your mind and heart with peace and hope that only He can give.

Hear my cry, O God;
    listen to my prayer.
From the ends of the earth I call to You,
    I call as my heart grows faint;
    lead me to the rock that is higher than I.
For You have been my refuge,
    a strong tower against the foe.
I long to dwell in Your tent forever
    and take refuge in the shelter of Your wings.
For You, God, have heard my vows;
    You have given me the heritage of those who fear Your name.
Increase the days of the king's life,
    his years for many generations.
May he be enthroned in God's presence forever;
    appoint Your love and faithfulness to protect him.
Then I will ever sing in praise of Your name
    and fulfill my vows day after day.

PSALM 61

ADORATION: The Bible reminds us that God is our shelter; He is our strong tower, where we can find protection from the enemy. Like a bird protects her child under her wing, He will cover us and keep us warm and safe throughout the night. Let us exalt Him for His goodness that brings us comfort.

CONFESSION: Ask God to reveal any sins in your heart, praying for His forgiveness and cleansing power. Ask Him to cultivate a heart of worship within you so that you will praise His name no matter what comes your way.

THANKSGIVING: Praise God for His love and faithfulness. Praise Him for His love and protection. Thank Him for the prayers He has answered, and for His constant presence.

SUPPLICATION: *Father, I cry out to You now for the strength I need to face my trials and tribulations, which, at times, overwhelm me. I trust You now to preserve and keep me in Your care and ask that You nourish my mind, body, and soul. Thank You for Your calming presence and never-ending love. All praise to You. Amen.*

Psalm 62

God's Word reminds us that we will never face troubles alone. Imagine waves crashing on a giant rock day after day, year after year. The waves keep coming, and the rock remains intact. Our Lord is like that rock—nothing moves Him. He is greater and stronger than any mountain of hurt or hardship we face. Even when we are undecisive or confused, we can look to God as our steady Savior, always reliable and true.

Tonight, turn and look away from your waves of worry—fix your focus on the Almighty God. He loves you and is your ever-present help in times of trouble. Call on Him, put your hope in Him, and wait patiently for His deliverance.

Truly my soul finds rest in God;
my salvation comes from Him.
Truly He is my rock and my salvation;
He is my fortress, I will never be shaken.
How long will you assault me?
Would all of you throw me down—
this leaning wall, this tottering fence?
Surely they intend to topple me
from my lofty place;
they take delight in lies.
With their mouths they bless,
but in their hearts they curse.
Yes, my soul, find rest in God;
my hope comes from Him.
Truly He is my rock and my salvation;
He is my fortress, I will not be shaken.
My salvation and my honor depend on God;
He is my mighty rock, my refuge.
Trust in Him at all times, you people;
pour out your hearts to Him,
for God is our refuge.
Surely the lowborn are but a breath,
the highborn are but a lie.
If weighed on a balance, they are nothing;
together they are only a breath.

Do not trust in extortion
*   or put vain hope in stolen goods;*
though your riches increase,
*   do not set your heart on them.*
One thing God has spoken,
*   two things I have heard:*
"Power belongs to You, God,
*   and with You, Lord, is unfailing love";*
and, "You reward everyone
*   according to what they have done."*

PSALM 62

ADORATION: This psalm says that God is our rock and our salvation. Can you trust Him and thank Him tonight for His steady love and constant presence? We can always find comfort in who God is, knowing our future is secure even if our present seems uncertain.

CONFESSION: Today's psalm reminds us that sometimes others will be against us. Think of a time you feared man, allowing your anxieties to take over. Take a moment to confess your lack of trust in God in that moment, asking Him to renew your trust in Him tonight.

THANKSGIVING: Praise God for His love and the salvation He offers to you today. Thank Him for being a God you can trust. Thank Him for the times He has given you rest when life was hard.

SUPPLICATION: Lord, I love Your Word and the reassurance and guidance it gives. Please be my rock tonight as I recover from the crashing waves I've faced today. Protect me from any lies I've believed about myself. Restore my soul and help me to find rest as I put my full and complete trust in You. In Jesus' name, I pray. Amen.

Psalm 63

We are bombarded with the promise of happiness through ads, promotions, and social media, all saying that our life would be better if only we did this or bought that. But the Bible—God's Word—reminds us we can only find true satisfaction in Him. Nothing we can buy or use compares to the ways He fills our hearts with lasting contentment and peace. No thing can or will ever measure up. He gave us life, and only He can fill it to the point of true satisfaction and joy.

As evening approaches, cast off the stress of the day, giving your thoughts and fears to the Lord. Turn your heart to praise—praise for God alone and nothing more. Let the peace He gives flow through your mind and spirit. For He alone is worthy.

You, God, are my God,
*   earnestly I seek You;*
I thirst for You,
*   my whole being longs for You,*
in a dry and parched land
*   where there is no water.*
I have seen You in the sanctuary
*   and beheld Your power and Your glory.*
Because Your love is better than life,
*   my lips will glorify You.*
I will praise You as long as I live,
*   and in Your name I will lift up my hands.*
I will be fully satisfied as with the richest of foods;
*   with singing lips my mouth will praise You.*
On my bed I remember You;
*   I think of You through the watches of the night.*
Because You are my help,
*   I sing in the shadow of Your wings.*
I cling to You;
*   Your right hand upholds me.*
Those who want to kill me will be destroyed;
*   they will go down to the depths of the earth.*
They will be given over to the sword

> *and become food for jackals.*
> *But the king will rejoice in God;*
> *all who swear by God will glory in Him,*
> *while the mouths of liars will be silenced.*

PSALM 63

ADORATION: Close your eyes and imagine a parched land thirsting for water to give it life. What was once a luscious land has now been reduced to dirt and dry ground. All the land can do is wait on its caretaker to water it. Like the parched land, you can only find satisfaction in the provision of your Creator. Let go of the things in this world and cling to God.

CONFESSION: Confess any times when you have placed your hope and trust in the things of the world rather than God. Ask for His forgiveness and ask Him to help you find satisfaction in Him alone.

THANKSGIVING: Rejoice in the strength and the power of the Lord. Thank Him for the love He has given you. Thank Him for the ways He has provided for you. Thank Him for the times He has protected you.

SUPPLICATION: *Lord, I confess I have tried to find fulfillment in things and other people, and it hasn't worked. I want to be so close to You that I know without a doubt that You provide all that I need. You are enough. Your love, Your presence, Your peace—there is none like You, and I feel grateful as I end this day and seek to rest in Your loving care. All glory and honor to You. Amen.*

Psalm 64

Knowing God's Word helps us face the many hard situations we have to endure in this world. Whether it's the people who oppose us and God or the circumstances that press in on every side, negative thoughts can tempt us to go astray or succumb to the darkness. But Scripture is our solid ground and defense. It is a double-edged sword for defending ourselves and standing firm in the face of trials. When we meditate on it, even memorize it, we maintain the advantage for winning each battle.

Tonight, we can dwell in God's safe place where nothing can harm us, where we can rest in His perfect peace. Let us meditate on His Word and trust in the Lord with all our hearts.

> God, hear my voice when I am in anguish.
> Protect my life from the terror of the enemy.
> Hide me from the scheming of wicked people,
> from the mob of evildoers,
> who sharpen their tongues like swords
> and aim bitter words like arrows,
> shooting from concealed places at the blameless.
> They shoot at him suddenly and are not afraid.
> They adopt an evil plan;
> they talk about hiding traps and say,
> "Who will see them?"
> They devise crimes and say,
> "We have perfected a secret plan."
> The inner man and the heart are mysterious.
> But God will shoot them with arrows;
> suddenly, they will be wounded.
> They will be made to stumble;
> their own tongues work against them.
> All who see them will shake their heads.
> Then everyone will fear
> and will tell about God's work,
> for they will understand what He has done.
> The righteous one rejoices in the Lord

and takes refuge in Him;
all those who are upright in heart
will offer praise.

PSALM 64 CSB

ADORATION: Take a deep breath in and imagine God's hands pulling you up, helping you rise above your enemies. Then as you exhale, imagine God striking down anything and anyone who tries to bring you down. Know you are safe and secure in Him. He will protect you throughout the night.

CONFESSION: Confess any times when you have tried to fight your battles in your own strength, in your own way. Pray that God will help you rely on the power of His Word to do what is right when others attack you. Pray He will help you forgive others like He forgives you.

THANKSGIVING: Rejoice in the name of the Lord. Thank Him for the times He has protected you and delivered you. Thank Him for the wonderful things He has done in your life.

SUPPLICATION: *Father, I pray now for the next time I am tempted to fight my own battle, that You will remind me to trust in and do as Your Word says. Help me to stop and listen to Your counsel and rely on Your strength and direction. Protect me tonight as I sleep; keep me in perfect peace as only You can do. In Your great name, I pray. Amen.*

Psalm 65

No matter what we're facing, there is always a reason to praise God—whether it's something big or something little, He has blessed us. One of the biggest sources of praise and awe is God's creation. Around the globe, His majesty is seen from the depths of the seas to the tops of snow-capped mountains; in the array of a beautiful bouquet to the hues of a summer sunset; in the song of a bird to the squeal of a child. God's Word reminds us He is our Creator and Provider, and we can find joy in Him as we soak in His glory.

No matter which kind of provision you need or when you need it, know God will sustain you through this night and into a new tomorrow. Let this psalm soothe your heart as you think of God's power and beauty as seen throughout creation.

God, You will be praised in Jerusalem.
  We will keep our promises to You.
You hear our prayers.
  All people will come to You.
Our guilt overwhelms us,
  but You forgive our sins.
Happy are the people You choose
  and invite to stay in Your court. . . .
You answer us in amazing ways,
  God our Savior.
People everywhere on the earth
  and beyond the sea trust You.
You made the mountains by Your strength;
  You are dressed in power.
You stopped the roaring seas . . .
  and the uproar of the nations. . . .
You take care of the land and water it;
  You make it very fertile.
The rivers of God are full of water.
  Grain grows because You make it grow. . . .
You soften the ground with rain,
  and then You bless it with crops.

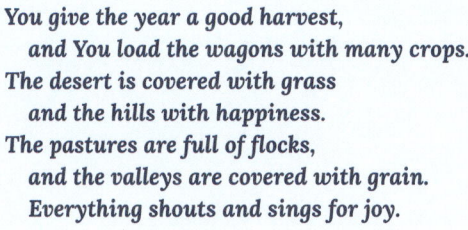

You give the year a good harvest,
    and You load the wagons with many crops.
The desert is covered with grass
    and the hills with happiness.
The pastures are full of flocks,
    and the valleys are covered with grain.
    Everything shouts and sings for joy.

PSALM 65:1-7, 9-13 NCV

ADORATION: Take a moment to meditate on the wonderful works of our Creator. Close your eyes and imagine the majestic mountains, the rolling hills, and the luscious meadows He created with His power and strength. Delight in the work of His hands. Know these same hands that created the roaring seas can calm the storms of your life. Worship Him now for His abundant blessings.

CONFESSION: Acknowledge your sins before the Lord and ask for His forgiveness. Ask for His help for resisting temptation in the future and in seeing the beauty all around you.

THANKSGIVING: Praise the Lord for His mercy and grace and think of a way you have seen His grace at work in your life. Thank Him for the prayers He has answered and for the blessings He has given you.

SUPPLICATION: *Lord, You provide so generously in ways that touch my life and bless my heart to the fullest. Thank You for Your creation and the beauty I get to enjoy every day. Help me not to get so busy or distracted with wanting things that don't satisfy. I want to recognize Your gifts of goodness and peace. Help me to be at rest in You tonight. In Christ, I pray. Amen.*

Psalm 66

Meditating on God's Word before we go to sleep can fill our hearts with joy and hope as it reminds us of everything God has done for those who love Him and are committed to Him. In tonight's psalm, we are reminded of God parting the waters so the Israelites could escape captivity. In the same way, as we turn to Him in our distress, He makes a way for us; His presence before our enemies causes them to cower and retreat. And He doesn't stop there! He goes on to fill our hearts with awe—His wonders never cease.

Take a moment now to quiet your mind and release all that stops you from experiencing God's glorious presence—any anger, hurt, offense, injustice, confusion. Allow His voice of truth to soften your spirit to receive the tender mercies He has for you. Let your heart, soul, and mind sing His praise and shout joyfully to Him.

> Let the whole earth shout joyfully to God!
> Sing about the glory of His name;
> make His praise glorious.
> Say to God, "How awe-inspiring are Your works!
> Your enemies will cringe before You
> because of Your great strength.
> The whole earth will worship You
> and sing praise to You.
> They will sing praise to Your name." Selah
> Come and see the wonders of God;
> His acts for humanity are awe-inspiring.
> He turned the sea into dry land,
> and they crossed the river on foot.
> There we rejoiced in Him. . . .
> For You, God, tested us;
> You refined us as silver is refined.
> You lured us into a trap;
> You placed burdens on our backs.
> You let men ride over our heads;
> we went through fire and water,
> but You brought us out to abundance. . . .

Come and listen, all who fear God,
and I will tell what He has done for me.
I cried out to Him with my mouth,
and praise was on my tongue. . . .
Blessed be God!
He has not turned away my prayer
or turned His faithful love from me.

PSALM 66:1-6, 10-12, 16-17, 20 CSB

ADORATION: Reflect on all the wondrous things God has done—not just in the Bible, but in your life. Take delight in His Word and His works. As you think about all He has done for you, let Him lighten your heart and ease your mind. Worship Him for His amazing goodness to you.

CONFESSION: Think of a time when God answered a prayer or blessed your life and you didn't take time to sincerely thank Him or maybe didn't even realize that it was an answered prayer or divine intervention. Acknowledge this and confess it, then take time to thank and glorify Him now.

THANKSGIVING: Rejoice in the name of the Lord. Praise Him for His wonderful deeds. Praise Him for His love and kindness toward you. Thank Him for the times He has helped you and delivered you. Thank Him for the prayers He has answered.

SUPPLICATION: *Lord, I come to You with a surrendered heart, relishing in Your blessings and thanking You for loving me in just the ways I need. I'm so grateful for the miraculous things You have done in my past and for the hope You give for my future. My heart is filled with joy, and my thoughts are filled with praise for You. Please hold me close and remind me of Your peace as I rest in Your arms. In Jesus' name. Amen.*

Psalm 67

Our God is the sovereign King who rules the nations, and He is the sovereign King with whom you have found favor. He promises to provide for and bless you with abundance. If the demands of the day make it hard to believe these promises, at the very least you can rest in knowing that you are secure in Him.

For tonight, He wants to bless you by lifting your burdens and giving you rest for your mind, body, and soul. Take a moment to stop and release all that you cling to other than Almighty God. Breathe in His blessing and favor. Breathe out your stress and anxiety. Surrender today's worries to the Lord and allow His Spirit to move in your heart and bring the comfort you so desire. He wants to pour out His blessing and favor upon you.

> *May God be gracious to us and bless us*
> *and make His face shine on us—*
> *so that Your ways may be known on earth,*
> *Your salvation among all nations.*
> *May the peoples praise You, God;*
> *may all the peoples praise You.*
> *May the nations be glad and sing for joy,*
> *for You rule the peoples with equity*
> *and guide the nations of the earth.*
> *May the peoples praise You, God;*
> *may all the peoples praise You.*
> *The land yields its harvest;*
> *God, our God, blesses us.*
> *May God bless us still,*
> *so that all the ends of the earth will fear Him.*

PSALM 67

ADORATION: Close your eyes and think about how God's gift of salvation is a love story that has unfolded throughout generations of people and of nations and throughout your life. Bow your heart before the Lord and let His joy fill your heart and renew your spirit. Bask in His presence and feel the light of His face shine upon you, keeping you warm and safe throughout the night. Ascribe to Him the praise and wonder due His name.

CONFESSION: Confess any doubts you have about God and His salvation, knowing He cares, and He is listening. Ask for His forgiveness and for His help to stay on His path of life and righteousness.

THANKSGIVING: Thank God for the blessings He has given you. Thank Him for the love and grace He has shown you, and for the promise of eternal life in heaven with Him.

SUPPLICATION: *Father, I thank You for the cleansing of my sin and the eternal life this allows. It is a gift I don't deserve, yet one I gladly accept. Help me to fully realize the height, depth, and width of Your love. Fill me with Your peace this night and help me to rest in the comfort You give. All glory and honor to You. Amen.*

Psalm 68

Tonight's psalm reminds us of the many ways God has used His power and strength to rescue, redeem, and restore His people. This is comforting because He exudes this same power in our lives today, including to those who are fatherless, widowed, homeless, and in prison. No one is left out of His hands of deliverance. We can put our trust in God and rest in His power and strength at any time, day or night.

As you surrender any anxious thoughts to God, know He is both capable and willing to bear your burdens because He loves you. Focus solely on Him now and meditate on His goodness. Listen for His still, small voice that speaks life and love into your mind, body, and soul.

> God arises. His enemies scatter,
> and those who hate Him flee from His presence. . . .
> Sing to God! Sing praises to His name.
> Exalt Him who rides on the clouds—
> His name is the LORD—and celebrate before Him.
> God in His holy dwelling is
> a father of the fatherless
> and a champion of widows.
> God provides homes for those who are deserted.
> He leads out the prisoners to prosperity,
> but the rebellious live in a scorched land. . . .
> God's chariots are tens of thousands,
> thousands and thousands;
> the Lord is among them in the sanctuary
> as He was at Sinai. . . .
> Blessed be the Lord!
> Day after day He bears our burdens;
> God is our salvation. Selah
> Our God is a God of salvation,
> and escape from death belongs to the LORD my Lord.
> Surely God crushes the heads of His enemies.
> the hairy brow of one who goes on in his guilty acts. . . .
> Your God has decreed your strength.

Show Your strength, God,
You who have acted on our behalf....
Sing to God, you kingdoms of the earth;
sing praise to the Lord, Selah
to Him who rides in the ancient, highest heavens.
Look, He thunders with His powerful voice!
Ascribe power to God.
His majesty is over Israel;
His power is among the clouds.
God, You are awe-inspiring in Your sanctuaries.
The God of Israel gives power and strength to His people.
Blessed be God!

PSALM 68:1, 4–6, 17, 19–21, 28, 32–35 CSB

ADORATION: Imagine God filling you with His power and strength, helping you overcome the darkness of the night. Allow Him to soothe your soul and rejuvenate your body. Visualize God as the sovereign King having compassion on you. Lift up your heart in worship and adoration for your mighty King.

CONFESSION: Acknowledge your sins before the Lord and ask for His forgiveness. Confess any doubts you have concerning God's power and strength. Ask Him to help you with your unbelief.

THANKSGIVING: Rejoice in the name of the Lord. Praise Him for His gift of salvation, mentioned in today's psalm. Thank Him for the ways He has provided for you. Thank Him for the times when He has protected you.

SUPPLICATION: *Father, it's so comforting to know that such a mighty God cares for me. Please help me to always remember to look to You first and seek Your power and strength in my times of need. Help me to point others who are vulnerable and oppressed to You for deliverance. Help me to rest easy tonight. In Jesus' name, I pray. Amen.*

Psalm 69

When the storms of life overwhelm us, the Bible says we will not be overtaken by the tumultuous waves because Jesus will rescue us. He understands our feelings of overwhelm because He faced difficult people and circumstances when He lived here on earth—He was scorned, mocked, and humiliated for all to see. But He was not defeated, and neither are we. In Him, we will find His love that sustains us and His grace that saves us. No matter what storm clouds seem to be hanging over our heads, we can know that God is with us, in the eye of the storm, holding us, comforting us through the night.

Reflect on the death of Jesus Christ on a cross, done out of love for you. Now think of Him in all His glory and power, sitting on the heavenly throne with His Father. Know you will share in the joy of His inheritance as you share in His suffering. His suffering will lead you to His salvation that He freely offers to you today. Allow His joy to lighten your heart and His hope to soothe your soul tonight.

Save me, God,
for the water has risen to my neck. . . .
I am weary from my crying;
my throat is parched. . . .
God, you know my foolishness,
and my guilty acts are not hidden from You. . . .
I have become a stranger to my brothers
and a foreigner to my mother's sons. . . .
Those who sit at the city gate talk about me,
and drunkards make up songs about me.
But as for me, Lord,
my prayer to You is for a time of favor.
In Your abundant, faithful love, God,
answer me with Your sure salvation. . . .
Answer me, Lord,
for Your faithful love is good.
In keeping with Your abundant compassion,
turn to me. . . .

You are aware of all my adversaries.
Insults have broken my heart,
and I am in despair. . . .
But as for me—poor and in pain—
let Your salvation protect me, God.
I will praise God's name with song
and exalt Him with thanksgiving. . . .
For the Lord listens to the needy
and does not despise
His own who are prisoners.
Let heaven and earth praise Him,
the seas and everything that moves in them,
for God will save Zion
and build up the cities of Judah.

PSALM 69:1, 3, 5, 8, 12-13, 16, 19-20, 29-30, 33-35 CSB

ADORATION: Even though the psalmist was "poor and in pain," he still exalted and praised God and looked to Him for help. He kept his eyes on the faithfulness of God even in troubling circumstances. Now, will we? Let us be glad and rejoice for He has kept His promises to us and shown us His greatness in our lives.

CONFESSION: Know that nothing is hidden from the Lord: He already knows your sins, and He has already forgiven you. But for your sake, it's vital to confess them and walk in God's grace.

THANKSGIVING: Rejoice in Lord and in the care and love He has for you. Praise His name. Thank Him for the times He has delivered you. Thank Him for His faithfulness in your life.

SUPPLICATION: *Lord, I call on You now—to rescue me from the numerous struggles I am facing. I look to You for strength and grace, compassion and help. I trust in You and place my life and my heart in Your hands for protection through this night. Thank You that I can rest safe and secure in peaceful sleep. With gratefulness, I pray. Amen.*

Psalm 70

When we find ourselves in a difficult situation, it's natural to want to call someone we trust for help and a listening ear. In these moments, we can call on Jesus, our perfect and trustworthy friend, who will listen anytime day or night. He *wants* us to cry out to Him, then release our cares to Him and wait for His deliverance. And even though waiting can be hard, we are not left to wait in nothingness—we can have His joy and hope to see us through.

As you prepare to read God's Word, ask Him to speak to you tonight. Ask for His truth to bring you comfort and peace as you prepare for sleep. Close your eyes and focus your thoughts on God; remember who He is, your Helper and Deliverer in times of trouble. He is the One who sustains you through the day and lifts your burdens at night.

Now take a deep breath and exhale your burdens into the care of Jesus. Let Him lift them from you and fill you with His peace that passes understanding. He is with you, and He cares. He is your greatest friend.

> Hasten, O God, to save me;
>   come quickly, LORD, to help me.
> May those who want to take my life
>   be put to shame and confusion;
> may all who desire my ruin
>   be turned back in disgrace.
> May those who say to me, "Aha! Aha!"
>   turn back because of their shame.
> But may all who seek You
>   rejoice and be glad in You;
> may those who long for Your saving help always say,
>   "The LORD is great!"
> But as for me, I am poor and needy;
>   come quickly to me, O God.
> You are my help and my deliverer;
>   LORD, do not delay.

PSALM 70

ADORATION: Imagine God delivering you from your troubles and the calm this brings to your mind. Let this image of God bearing your burdens soak deep into your heart. He loves you and is always with you to help and guide you through difficult seasons. Now receive the joy that is yours through His Spirit, and praise His holy name.

CONFESSION: We tend to praise God for what He does rather than for who He is. God is good, goodness is who He is. Confess any doubts you have of His goodness. Ask Him to help you focus on who He is rather than on what He does for you.

THANKSGIVING: Praise the name of the Lord. Praise Him for His glory and power. Thank Him for the times He has helped you and delivered you.

SUPPLICATION: *Lord, I open my heart to You now and cast my anxieties at Your feet. I don't know what to do, but my eyes are on You. I know You love me and are for me, now help me to fully embrace this truth. Sustain me, fill me with Your strength, deliver me, and protect me as I sleep. Restore my soul as I face a new day tomorrow in the power and strength that is mine, all because of You. In Jesus' name, I pray. Amen.*

Psalm 71

No matter what age you are, God sustains you for exactly what you need for the season you're in. When you see how God has sustained you throughout the ups and downs of life, it is natural to tell others of what He has done. As today's psalm explains, praising God becomes the natural outpouring of your heart as you see God's blessings all around you.

Tonight, meditate on these powerful verses from Psalm 71. Think about the way the psalmist "tells," "proclaims," and even "sings" of God's wonderful works.

In You, LORD, I have taken refuge;
let me never be put to shame. . . .
Be my rock of refuge,
to which I can always go;
give the command to save me, . . .
For You have been my hope, Sovereign LORD,
my confidence since my youth.
From birth I have relied on You; . . .

My mouth will tell of Your righteous deeds,
of Your saving acts all day long—
though I know not how to relate them all.
I will come and proclaim Your mighty acts, Sovereign LORD;
I will proclaim Your righteous deeds, Yours alone.
Since my youth, God, You have taught me,
and to this day I declare Your marvelous deeds.
Even when I am old and gray,
do not forsake me, my God,
till I declare Your power to the next generation,
Your mighty acts to all who are to come.
Your righteousness, God, reaches to the heavens,
You who have done great things.
Who is like you, God?
Though You have made me see troubles,
many and bitter,
You will restore my life again;

from the depths of the earth
You will again bring me up....
My lips will shout for joy
when I sing praise to You—
I whom You have delivered.
My tongue will tell of Your righteous acts
all day long,
for those who wanted to harm me
have been put to shame and confusion.

PSALM 71:1, 3, 5-6, 15-20, 23-24

ADORATION: Thinking of all the wonderful ways God has been faithful in your life is an excellent way to calm your mind as you prepare to sleep. Let the joy of His presence and of His marvelous deeds lighten your heart. Praise Him as you rest peacefully through the night.

CONFESSION: Think of a time when you took credit for something rather than giving the glory to God and ask for His forgiveness. Ask Him to help you turn to Him in praise more often.

THANKSGIVING: Rejoice in the righteousness and calming presence of the Lord. Praise Him for His goodness and faithfulness. Thank Him for the wonderful things He has done in your life and for being the One you can always count on.

SUPPLICATION: *Lord, I lift all of my fears and worries to You tonight. Please help me to find Your peace and remain there. Help me to be a mouthpiece that passionately declares Your marvelous deeds and wonderous works. Lighten my heart, mind, and soul now as I lay my head down and rest. As I sleep, please restore my body for a new day. All glory to You, I pray. Amen.*

Psalm 72

Although there will always be injustice in the world, we can also look ahead and cling to hope as we anticipate the future reign of Christ. We can look forward to the day when He will wipe away our tears and our pain, and suffering will be no more. The brightness of our future with Christ can quell any anxiety over our present.

Our glorious future with God is reason enough to remain hopeful tonight. Embrace this truth as you read and meditate on tonight's psalm.

Endow the king with Your justice, O God,
the royal son with Your righteousness.
May he judge Your people in righteousness,
Your afflicted ones with justice.
May the mountains bring prosperity to the people,
the hills the fruit of righteousness.
May he defend the afflicted among the people
and save the children of the needy;
may he crush the oppressor.
May he endure as long as the sun,
as long as the moon, through all generations.
May he be like rain falling on a mown field,
like showers watering the earth.
In his days may the righteous flourish
and prosperity abound till the moon is no more.
May he rule from sea to sea
and from the River to the ends of the earth.
May the desert tribes bow before him
and his enemies lick the dust. . . .
For he will deliver the needy who cry out,
the afflicted who have no one to help.
He will take pity on the weak and the needy
and save the needy from death.
He will rescue them from oppression and violence,
for precious is their blood in his sight. . . .
Praise be to the LORD God, the God of Israel,
who alone does marvelous deeds.

Praise be to His glorious name forever;
may the whole earth be filled with His glory.
Amen and Amen.

PSALM 72:1-9, 12-14, 18-19

ADORATION: God promises to lift up the poor and the needy, the weak and the vulnerable, to administer His justice—and we all fall into those categories. Praise Him that we can know victory and be set free from our fears and worries.

CONFESSION: Confess any times when you did not stand up for God's justice in your community. Pray He will fill your heart with compassion for the poor and the needy, for the oppressed and the vulnerable.

THANKSGIVING: Praise His name, rejoicing in His power and glory. Rejoice in His strength. Thank Him for His hope and peace. Thank Him for the opportunity to spend eternity with Him.

SUPPLICATION: *Father, I'm so grateful that I can trust You with the plans You have for my life. Thank You for the promise of a bright, eternal future with You. Help me until that time to stand firm and act when I see injustice around me. Help me to stay on Your path of righteousness, where I can rest safely and securely through this night and into a new day. In Jesus' name, I pray. Amen.*

Psalm 73

When we live for personal gain and applause, we aren't truly fully satisfied. This is because worldly possessions and positions of power bring only temporal pleasures and prosperity; they never bring true satisfaction.

Tonight, remember your world possessions are temporary, but that the inheritance of the Lord is forever. And what He has in store for you in heaven is far greater than anything you can imagine. He keeps you safe and secure; His strength sustains you. Fix your mind on finding the joy and hope in Him as you immerse yourself in God's truth.

God is indeed good to Israel,
to the pure in heart.
But as for me, my feet almost slipped;
my steps nearly went astray.
For I envied the arrogant;
I saw the prosperity of the wicked.
They have an easy time until they die,
and their bodies are well fed.
They are not in trouble like others;
they are not afflicted like most people.
Therefore, pride is their necklace,
and violence covers them like a garment. . . .
Look at them—the wicked!
They are always at ease,
and they increase their wealth. . . .
When I tried to understand all this,
it seemed hopeless
until I entered God's sanctuary.
Then I understood their destiny.
Indeed, You put them in slippery places;
You make them fall into ruin. . . .
When I became embittered
and my innermost being was wounded, . . .
Yet I am always with You;
You hold my right hand.

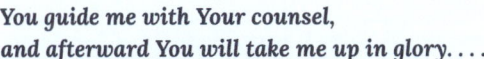

You guide me with Your counsel,
and afterward You will take me up in glory....

Those far from You will certainly perish;
You destroy all who are unfaithful to You.
But as for me, God's presence is my good.
I have made the Lord God my refuge,
so I can tell about all You do.

PSALM 73:1-6, 12, 16-18, 21, 23-24, 27-28 CSB

ADORATION: When you feel like others are prospering and you aren't, turning to God can help alleviate your frustrations and jealousy as He shifts your temporal perspective to an eternal one. You can find hope in the eternal rewards that await you in heaven. Exalt the Lord for being the deepest fulfillment you could ever experience on earth.

CONFESSION: Think of a time when you were envious of a person's wealth and lifestyle, confessing any jealousy in your heart. Ask God to help you value Him and His Word above all else.

THANKSGIVING: Praise God for His wonderful deeds. Praise Him for His faithfulness. Thank Him for His provision in the present and future.

SUPPLICATION: *Father, being surrounded by worldly grandeur is not easy—I do, at times, become tempted and lured by what appears to be a good direction. Help me to stay on the path You have for me and be completely content. I want Your Spirit to be my guide and to fill me in ways I know that the things in this life here cannot fulfill. I open my heart and keep my mind focused on You and the eternal gain I have, all because of Your Son. Thank You for such a gift. Amen.*

Psalm 74

When we face difficulty in our lives, it is easy to focus on the losses in our present rather than the victories in our past. In these moments of struggle, the Bible tells us to reflect on the times the Lord has delivered us and hold on to the hope that He will help us at just the right time.

Take a moment to close your eyes and remember what God has done for you. Hold on to those memories with full assurance that He is always with you, upholding you and sustaining you. Trust with all of your heart that He will help you now and in your future, just as He has done in your past. He is for you, not against you. He loves you, and He cares. Breathe in His power and strength. Breathe out your stress and anxiety from today as you meditate on His Word.

> Why have You rejected us forever, God?
> Why does Your anger burn
> against the sheep of Your pasture?
> Remember Your congregation,
> which You purchased long ago
> and redeemed as the tribe for Your own possession.
> Remember Mount Zion where You dwell.
> Make Your way to the perpetual ruins,
> to all that the enemy has destroyed in the sanctuary....
> God, how long will the enemy mock?
> Will the foe insult Your name forever?
> Why do You hold back Your hand?
> Stretch out Your right hand and destroy them!
> God my King is from ancient times,
> performing saving acts on the earth.
> You divided the sea with Your strength;
> You smashed the heads of the sea monsters in the water;
> You crushed the heads of Leviathan;
> You fed him to the creatures of the desert.
> You opened up springs and streams;
> You dried up ever-flowing rivers.
> The day is Yours, also the night;

You established the moon and the sun.
You set all the boundaries of the earth;
You made summer and winter. . . .
Do not let the oppressed turn away in shame;
let the poor and needy praise Your name.
Rise up, God, champion Your cause!

PSALM 74:1–3, 10–17, 21–22 CSB

ADORATION: Meditating on the mighty deeds of the Lord can help lift your spirit and bring you hope to comfort you through the night. Knowing anything is possible with God will put your mind at ease. Take a moment to worship Him now for consoling and comforting your heart and rest in the relief this gives. His goodness is never-ending!

CONFESSION: Confess the times when you've let your mind focus on your problems more than the ways God has helped and redeemed your life. Ask for His forgiveness. Allow His mercy and love to wash over you and release any guilt and shame you are carrying.

THANKSGIVING: Rejoice in the hope of the Lord, offered to you tonight. Praise Him for His power and strength. Thank Him for the times He has helped you and delivered you. Thank Him for the ways He is faithful in your life.

SUPPLICATION: *Lord, I turn to You tonight in full faith that You are working on my behalf in all my circumstances, even if I can't see what You're doing. I know this because of what You have done in my past; may I never forget Your goodness and power. Give me patience to wait on Your perfect timing. Deliver me from the anxiety I hold on to. Increase my faith so I can be in perfect peace as I go to sleep. In the palm of Your hand is where I want to be. All glory to You. Amen.*

Psalm 75

Tonight's psalm reminds us that God is the final judge of *everything*. His Word says He will judge in His time, and He promises to be fair. Sometimes we want to handle unjust matters on our own, but He clearly says He will overthrow those who seek to harm and destroy us. It is our job to surrender to Him what is not ours to handle, and when we do, unwanted anxiety and worry immediately melt away, and we are free to truly rest in God's presence.

Take a deep breath and imagine God's Spirit flowing through you. Breathe out and release the things you're clinging to that are not yours to carry. He is the sovereign King who rules with His love, compassion, and peace, not just in biblical times, but right now in your life and circumstances.

> We praise You, God,
>> we praise You, for Your Name is near;
>> people tell of Your wonderful deeds.
> You say, "I choose the appointed time;
>> it is I who judge with equity.
> When the earth and all its people quake,
>> it is I who hold its pillars firm.
> To the arrogant I say, 'Boast no more,'
>> and to the wicked, 'Do not lift up your horns.
> Do not lift your horns against heaven;
>> do not speak so defiantly.'"
> No one from the east or the west
>> or from the desert can exalt themselves.
> It is God who judges:
>> He brings one down, He exalts another.
> In the hand of the LORD is a cup
>> full of foaming wine mixed with spices;
> He pours it out, and all the wicked of the earth
>> drink it down to its very dregs.
> As for me, I will declare this forever;
>> I will sing praise to the God of Jacob,

who says, "I will cut off the horns of all the wicked,
but the horns of the righteous will be lifted up."

PSALM 75

ADORATION: In the end, God will cast the final judgment. We will join Him in heaven, where we will spend eternity. Tonight, let's find hope for our future and rest for our present. No matter how dark your nights are, know the light of the Lord is shining upon you even now.

CONFESSION: Think of a time when you doubted the wisdom of God's timing and tried to take matters into your own hands. Confess your doubts and your fears of putting your trust in God. Ask for His forgiveness. Ask Him to help you trust His timing and trust Him to judge fairly.

THANKSGIVING: Rejoice in the sovereignty of the Lord. Thank Him for being a righteous judge who shows mercy to you and also holds the wicked in this world accountable. Thank Him for the ways He has shown you mercy in your life.

SUPPLICATION: *Father, You are a great and mighty God, and I ask that You give me the faith I need to know without a doubt that You are aware of the injustice I see, and You will address it in Your perfect time and way. Lead me away from the temptation to speak or act out of turn—I want to be in Your will at all times. Protect me this night and help me to rest secure in Your peace. Renew and refresh my body, mind, and spirit as I sleep. In Jesus' name, I pray. Amen.*

Psalm 76

God is not only our Creator, but He is also our Judge. He judges in compassion and love over the earth, humanity, and our very lives. His eyes see everything. Nothing slides by or escapes His attention. He also knows man's heart and the motives in which we do what we do.

He will judge fairly and accurately all the injustice He sees. We never have to worry about facing our troubles or injustice done against us alone—He is present and at work. We can all find comfort in the powerful presence of our sovereign Lord. Let us remember that He will protect and sustain us through the night.

God is renowned in Judah;
in Israel His name is great.
His tent is in Salem,
His dwelling place in Zion.
There He broke the flashing arrows,
the shields and the swords, the weapons of war.
You are radiant with light,
more majestic than mountains rich with game.
The valiant lie plundered,
they sleep their last sleep;
not one of the warriors
can lift his hands.
At Your rebuke, God of Jacob,
both horse and chariot lie still.
It is You alone who are to be feared.
Who can stand before You when You are angry?
From heaven You pronounced judgment,
and the land feared and was quiet—
when You, God, rose up to judge,
to save all the afflicted of the land.
Surely Your wrath against mankind brings You praise,
and the survivors of Your wrath are restrained.
Make vows to the LORD your God and fulfill them;
let all the neighboring lands

> *bring gifts to the One to be feared.*
> *He breaks the spirit of rulers;*
> *He is feared by the kings of the earth.*

PSALM 76

ADORATION: Meditating on the power and strength of the Lord can put our minds at ease and help us experience deep, restful peace tonight. His power can strike down our fears, and His strength can carry our burdens so that we may find rest. Praise Him for the comfort this brings.

CONFESSION: Think of a time you made a vow to the Lord and did not fulfill it. When have you forgotten to thank Him for an answered prayer or a resolve to a difficult situation or struggle? Confess any sins before Him. Ask for His forgiveness. Pray He will help you be faithful and keep your commitments to Him.

THANKSGIVING: Rejoice in the power and the strength of the Lord. Give God the glory for the wonderful things He has done in your life. Thank Him for His protection and provision. Thank Him for His justice that He brings to our world.

SUPPLICATION: *Lord God, I look to You now and give thanks to You for Your greatness over all my circumstances. I put my full trust in Your power and commitment to be slow to anger and to judge fairly. Please give me patience and wisdom as I wait for Your will to unfold not only for this world, but in my life. I turn to You and You alone for rest for my soul as this day draws to a close. All glory and honor to You. Amen.*

Psalm 77

Life can sometimes hit us hard, leaving us overwhelmed and doubting that God will provide refuge. The psalmist in tonight's reading portrays this emotional roller coaster, but his cries are interspersed with his proclamations of faith. We can model this same communication with God in the midst of our struggles. God wants to hear us speak openly and honestly about our fears and struggles. His mercy and compassion, His power and presence are ours to receive when we place our worries at His feet.

Take a moment to lift up your cares to God. Allow yourself to be comforted by the loving Lord. Allow Him to refresh you and rejuvenate you tonight.

> I cried out to God for help;
>> I cried out to God to hear me.
> When I was in distress, I sought the Lord; . . .
> I thought about the former days,
>> the years of long ago;
> I remembered my songs in the night.
>> My heart meditated and my spirit asked: . . .
> "Has God forgotten to be merciful?
>> Has He in anger withheld His compassion?"
> Then I thought, "To this I will appeal:
>> the years when the Most High stretched out His right hand.
> I will remember the deeds of the LORD;
>> yes, I will remember Your miracles of long ago." . . .
> Your thunder was heard in the whirlwind,
>> Your lightning lit up the world;
>> the earth trembled and quaked.
> Your path led through the sea,
>> Your way through the mighty waters,
>> though Your footprints were not seen.
> You led Your people like a flock
>> by the hand of Moses and Aaron.

PSALM 77:1–2, 5–6, 9–11, 18–20

ADORATION: As you lie down to sleep, consider the works of the Lord in your life and meditate on His mighty deeds of the past to find hope and peace for your soul now. May His works be a reminder of His power and strength. Worship Him for His constant love.

CONFESSION: Think of a time when you doubted God's faithfulness, confessing any fears and doubts you have tonight. Ask Him to remind you of His wondrous works when you have doubts. Ask Him to help you put your trust in Him when trouble comes your way.

THANKSGIVING: Rejoice in the goodness and the faithfulness of the Lord. Praise Him for His mighty deeds. Thank Him for the ways He was worked on your behalf. Give Him the glory for any miracles He has performed in your life.

SUPPLICATION: *Father, I cry out to You tonight and lay my struggles and troubles at Your feet. I will wait expectantly for Your presence to fill me with Your calm and serenity. Guide me with Your wisdom and help me to trust You even when I don't understand Your plans. Give me patience as I wait for Your direction. Until then, I keep my eyes on You and receive Your perfect peace through this night. With a grateful heart, I pray. Amen.*

Psalm 78

God is faithful to us even when we are unfaithful. Isn't that amazing? God has unfailing love and compassion for His people. But there's even more to it: He relentlessly pursues His people. He knows exactly where we are and what we're going through at any given time. And when we seek Him, He will guide us by day and night, and rescue us and restore us with His protection and provision. He fills us with His hope for tomorrow and helps us find rest in Him tonight.

My people, hear my instruction;
listen to the words from my mouth.
I will declare wise sayings; . . .
We will not hide them from their children,
but will tell a future generation
the praiseworthy acts of the LORD, . . .
so that they might put their confidence in God
and not forget God's works,
but keep His commands. . . .
They forgot what He had done,
the wondrous works He had shown them.
He worked wonders in the sight of their ancestors . . .
He split the sea and brought them across; . . .
He led them with a cloud by day
and with a fiery light throughout the night.
He split rocks in the wilderness
and gave them drink as abundant as the depths. . . .
Despite all this, they kept sinning
and did not believe His wondrous works. . . .
Yet He was compassionate;
He atoned for their iniquity
and did not destroy them. . . .
He brought them to His holy territory, . . .
He drove out nations before them. . . .
He chose David His servant
and took him from the sheep pens;
He brought him from tending ewes

to be shepherd over His people Jacob—
over Israel, His inheritance.
He shepherded them with a pure heart
and guided them with his skillful hands.

PSALM 78:1-2, 4, 7, 11-15, 32, 38, 54-55, 70-72 CSB

ADORATION: Reflecting on all the wondrous works of the Lord throughout history and throughout our lives reminds us we serve a compassionate, loving Father. His Word is like manna coming down from heaven, fulfilling our needs, sustaining us, and fueling our mind, body, and soul. Let us praise Him for His goodness.

CONFESSION: Think of a time when you lost faith and hope in God, confessing any doubts you have of God's goodness and faithfulness still. Ask for His forgiveness, knowing that He loves you.

THANKSGIVING: Rejoice in the power and strength of the Lord. Praise Him for His provision and protection. Thank Him for His faithfulness in your life even when you haven't been faithful in return.

SUPPLICATION: *Father, give me the mind to remember all that You have done for me—there is too much to recount. Give me the courage to live out my life as You lead with a heart full of trust in You. Thank You for Your faithfulness. Cover me with Your peace. Watch over me now as I enter into rest for the night. In Jesus' name. Amen.*

Psalm 79

When we see injustice in this world, we can be tempted to remedy it on our own. But the Lord is far more just and righteous than us, and He has a grander plan for redemption. We can lament to God and vent our honest thoughts, but for our souls to find true rest from difficult circumstances around us, we must bring the injustices we see around us to Him and declare our praise for His mighty and righteous judgment. Proclaim your trust in Him and allow His peace to fill your heart, offering you respite and renewal.

O God, the nations have invaded Your inheritance;
    they have defiled Your holy temple, . . .
They have left the dead bodies of Your servants
    as food for the birds of the sky, . . .
We are objects of contempt to our neighbors,
    of scorn and derision to those around us.
How long, LORD? Will You be angry forever?
    How long will Your jealousy burn like fire?
Pour out Your wrath on the nations
    that do not acknowledge You,
on the kingdoms
    that do not call on Your name;
for they have devoured Jacob
    and devastated his homeland. . . .
Help us, God our Savior,
    for the glory of Your name;
deliver us and forgive our sins
    for Your name's sake. . . .
May the groans of the prisoners come before You;
    with Your strong arm preserve those condemned to die.
Pay back into the laps of our neighbors seven times
    the contempt they have hurled at You, Lord.
Then we Your people, the sheep of Your pasture,
    will praise You forever;

from generation to generation
we will proclaim Your praise.

PSALM 79:1-2, 4-7, 9, 11-13

ADORATION: Take some time to meditate on the sovereignty of the Lord. Know without a doubt that His justice *will* prevail. Allow this truth to give you rest tonight and hope for your future. Worship Him and give Him glory for the comfort this brings.

CONFESSION: Think of a time when you didn't place your trust in God's sovereignty and justice, asking for His forgiveness. Ask for Him to help you be patient and wait on Him to make things right in your life and in the world.

THANKSGIVING: Rejoice in the fact that He has great kindness and love for you! Thank Him for His great mercy and love. Thank Him for the times He has helped you and delivered you. Thank Him for His perfect justice He brings to the world.

SUPPLICATION: *Father God, as the psalmist says, "How long, Yahweh?" How long will You let injustice continue and expect me to sit idly by? It's hard not to act on my own, yet I will wait on You. I pray for Your mercy to reign and Your compassion to be ever present in my life and in this world. Protect and keep me in Your perfect peace tonight. Restore my soul as I surrender into Your loving hands of grace. In Jesus' name. Amen.*

Psalm 80

God's Word reminds us that He will save and restore us in every situation—He will not leave us in our brokenness. And even more, He will use our brokenness to draw us to His path of hope and salvation where our future is secure and where we can find rest. He can restore anything we see as ruined; He can redeem anything that's been lost. He is a God who brings healing to the worst of wounds and hope into the darkest of times.

Tonight, surrender your troubles and cast your burdens onto the One who is capable of taking them all and working them for your good. Breathe in God's life-giving power and exhale all that seems lost. Relax in knowing He loves you with an everlasting love.

> Please listen, O Shepherd of Israel,
>> You who lead Joseph's descendants like a flock.
> O God, enthroned above the cherubim,
>> display Your radiant glory
>> to Ephraim, Benjamin, and Manasseh.
> Show us Your mighty power.
>> Come to rescue us! . . .
> Turn us again to Yourself, O God of Heaven's Armies.
>> Make Your face shine down upon us.
>> Only then will we be saved.
> You brought us from Egypt like a grapevine;
>> You drove away the pagan nations and
> transplanted us into Your land.
> You cleared the ground for us,
>> and we took root and filled the land.
> Our shade covered the mountains;
>> our branches covered the mighty cedars. . . .
> But now, why have You broken down our walls
>> so that all who pass by may steal our fruit? . . .
> Come back, we beg You, O God of Heaven's Armies.
>> Look down from heaven and see our plight.
> Take care of this grapevine
>> that You Yourself have planted,

> *this son You have raised for Yourself....*
> *Turn us again to Yourself, O LORD God of Heaven's Armies.*
> *Make Your face shine down upon us.*
> *Only then will we be saved.*

PSALM 80:1-2, 7-10, 12, 14-15, 19 NLT

ADORATION: Like lost sheep in the wilderness, we need our Good Shepherd to lead us, guiding us into safety. When we call upon His name, He will gather us to Him and drive us from the barren wilderness into the green pastures where we can once again experience His hope, peace, and joy.

CONFESSION: Think of a time when you turned away from God and followed your own path. Confess this to the Lord and ask for His forgiveness and mercy. Turn to Him to guide you down His path of life and righteousness.

THANKSGIVING: Praise God for His faithfulness during times when you've been rebellious. Thank Him for redeeming you and restoring you. Rejoice in the promising and hopeful future you have in Him.

SUPPLICATION: *Thank You, Father, for not leaving me during times when I've strayed from You. Thank You for covering me with Your love when I didn't always do or go where You've led. Your presence and forgiveness bring such comfort to my heart and allow me to receive the peace that only You can give. In Your great name, I pray. Amen.*

Psalm 81

When we face challenges, it can be hard not to try to solve our problems on our own rather than turn to God for His guidance. In His mercy, He understands our struggle with this and continually reminds us in His Word about the incredible blessings that await when we listen to His leading and trust in His ways. He longs to bless us as He waits for us to surrender to Him.

Tonight, open your palms and prepare to receive His blessing as you release your problems into His hands. Let His peace fill your heart and His amazing love be real to you.

Sing for joy to God our strength;
shout in triumph to the God of Jacob.
Lift up a song—play the tambourine,
the melodious lyre, and the harp....
For this is a statute for Israel,
an ordinance of the God of Jacob....
You called out in distress, and I rescued you;
I answered you from the thundercloud....
Listen, my people, and I will admonish you.
Israel, if you would only listen to Me!
There must not be a strange god among you;
you must not bow down to a foreign god.
I am the LORD your God,
who brought you up from the land of Egypt.
Open your mouth wide, and I will fill it.
"But My people did not listen to My voice;
Israel did not obey Me.
So I gave them over to their stubborn hearts
to follow their own plans.
If only My people would listen to Me
and Israel would follow My ways,
I would quickly subdue their enemies
and turn my hand against their foes."...
But He would feed Israel with the best wheat.
"I would satisfy you with honey from the rock."

PSALM 81:1-2, 4, 7-14, 16 CSB

ADORATION: Meditate on the wonderful works of the Lord and His unwavering faithfulness, as demonstrated in this psalm. Remember the times He has protected you, even when your heart was far away from Him. Exalt Him for how He continually wants to bless you with His provision and peace. Let your mind, body, and soul rest in His presence.

CONFESSION: Acknowledge any doubts you have concerning God's power and provision, asking Him for His forgiveness in these doubts. Pray you will be able to put your trust in Him and follow His leading in your life today.

THANKSGIVING: Praise God for His faithfulness, thanking Him for the times He has been faithful in your life even when you have not always been faithful to Him. Praise Him for His mercy. Thank Him for the blessings He has given you.

SUPPLICATION: *Father, thank You for Your steadfast love, even during times when I try to handle my problems on my own. Please keep me close to You and restore me to Your joy as I release my anxieties and cares to You. Help my mind and heart to remain focused on Your promises and faithfulness to me throughout my life. Tonight, I lay me down and rest in complete trust, of which You alone are worthy. All glory to You. Amen.*

Psalm 82

Focusing on the brokenness in our world can overwhelm our spirits and make our hearts heavy with anger and sadness. In these moments, it's vital to remember that God is sovereign over all the nations and their leaders. Our most important role is to pray for justice and restoration and to love those who have been victimized, leaving the final consequences in His hands.

Tonight, let us receive strength from God's Word to stand up for what is right in His eyes and find rest for our souls as we submit to Him and His ways.

God presides in the great assembly;

> He renders judgment among the "gods":
> "How long will you defend the unjust
>   and show partiality to the wicked?
> Defend the weak and the fatherless;
>   uphold the cause of the poor and the oppressed.
> Rescue the weak and the needy;
>   deliver them from the hand of the wicked.
> "The 'gods' know nothing, they understand nothing.
>   They walk about in darkness;
>   all the foundations of the earth are shaken.
> "I said, 'You are "gods";
>   you are all sons of the Most High.'
> But you will die like mere mortals;
>   you will fall like every other ruler."
> Rise up, O God, judge the earth,
>   for all the nations are Your inheritance.

PSALM 82

ADORATION: Meditate on the mercy and justice of the Lord and what it means for your life tonight. Picture Him as a righteous judge who perfectly rules over the earth with fairness and equity. He sees every injustice and casts judgment in His righteousness and in His truth. One day there will be accountability for all who defended the unjust and showed partiality to the wicked. Find comfort in the hope of God's redemption of His world and restoration of His justice.

CONFESSION: Think of a time when you committed a wrong and received grace from God instead of consequences you thought would occur. Determine to remember this the next time you are tempted to carry out justice on your own.

THANKSGIVING: Praise God for His mercy and justice, rejoicing in His sovereignty. Thank Him for the times when He has made things right in your life and in our world.

SUPPLICATION: *Lord, I see injustice all around me, and I want to help in ways that honor You. Give me wisdom and discernment when making judgment calls in my mind. Help me to remember Your grace in my life and that, in the end, You are the One to act justly over all of humanity. Please unburden my heart now and give me rest tonight, knowing the world is in Your hands. Fill me with Your peace as I turn to You. In Jesus' name, I pray. Amen.*

Psalm 83

Tonight's psalmist understood the common temptation to want to fight back against those who conspire against us and inspires us to be honest about our struggles and temptations with wanting to solve our problems on our own instead of giving them to the Lord. Even though we're supposed to pray for our enemies, it's hard not to want to fight back if for no other reason than to satisfy our own need to act.

But when foes rise against us, we can rest assured that God is with us to help us fight our battles, and His ways are always best. We can find comfort knowing we never have to face adversity alone and that He is still in control. As you prepare to read tonight's psalm, take a moment to lift any harbored resentment or anger against others to God. Clear your mind of any distractions and focus on hearing His voice through His Word.

O God, do not remain silent;
   do not turn a deaf ear,
   do not stand aloof, O God.
See how Your enemies growl,
   how Your foes rear their heads.
With cunning they conspire against Your people;
   they plot against those You cherish. . . .
With one mind they plot together;
   they form an alliance against You. . . .
Even Assyria has joined them
   to reinforce Lot's descendants.
Do to them as You did to Midian,
   as You did to Sisera and Jabin at the river Kishon,
who perished at Endor
   and became like dung on the ground. . . .
Make them like tumbleweed, my God,
   like chaff before the wind.
As fire consumes the forest
   or a flame sets the mountains ablaze,
so pursue them with Your tempest
   and terrify them with Your storm.
Cover their faces with shame, LORD,

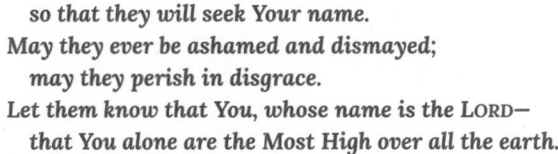

so that they will seek Your name.
May they ever be ashamed and dismayed;
    may they perish in disgrace.
Let them know that You, whose name is the LORD—
    that You alone are the Most High over all the earth.

PSALM 83:1-3, 5, 8-10, 13-18

ADORATION: Think about how powerful and Almighty God is, taking joy in knowing and serving this Almighty God. Invite His presence to be near to you as you wind down the day. Find comfort in knowing you serve the one, true God who controls all of the earth.

CONFESSION: Think of a tumultuous time when you did not trust God to work for your good. Confess any doubts you have of God's power and any fear of others you are holding on to. Ask Him to help you focus on and turn to Him when you need help.

THANKSGIVING: Thank God for the ways in which He's protected and delivered you through a difficult time. Thank Him, in advance, for the ways in which He will continue to help you and for the times when He will deliver you in the future.

SUPPLICATION: *Lord, You know my heart, and I ask You to move in my life in a mighty way. Rise against those who rise against me, and help me remember that I am secure in Your hands. I trust in You, and look to You for peace. I praise Your holy name. Amen.*

Psalm 84

While we are here on earth, there will always be a longing in our hearts. We can try to fill it with success, things, or people, but this longing is for God and is only satisfied by Him. Nothing on this earth can compare to the fullness and glory of entering His courts and dwelling in the glory of His presence.

Tonight, ask God to fill your heart with His presence, the presence of the living God. He is alive in you, constantly working to bless you with a glimpse of heaven within your life here on earth. We have a beautiful and glorious home in which we'll see Him face-to-face, but until then, we can enter His presence through His Word.

How lovely is Your dwelling place,
   Lord Almighty!
My soul yearns, even faints,
   for the courts of the Lord;
my heart and my flesh cry out
   for the living God.
Even the sparrow has found a home,
   and the swallow a nest for herself,
   where she may have her young—
a place near Your altar,
   Lord Almighty, my King and my God.
Blessed are those who dwell in Your house;
   they are ever praising You.
Blessed are those whose strength is in You,
   whose hearts are set on pilgrimage. . . .
They go from strength to strength,
   till each appears before God in Zion.
Hear my prayer, Lord God Almighty;
   listen to me, God of Jacob.
Look on our shield, O God;
   look with favor on Your anointed one.
Better is one day in Your courts
   than a thousand elsewhere; . . .
For the Lord God is a sun and shield;
   the Lord bestows favor and honor;

no good thing does He withhold
from those whose walk is blameless.
LORD *Almighty,*
blessed is the one who trusts in You.

PSALM 84:1–5, 7–12

ADORATION: Take a moment to reflect on the glory of God and what it means for your life here on earth. His light shines bright like the sun, dispelling the darkness that surrounds you. Imagine His love reaching the depths of your soul and filling it with joy and peace to the brim. Sit in His presence and find satisfaction for your soul in the living God.

CONFESSION: Confess your longing and need for God. Ask for His strength and grace to help you overcome any sin that hinders you from experiencing His glory.

THANKSGIVING: Rejoice in the strength and the glory you have in the Lord. Thank God for pouring out His blessing and favor upon you. Thank Him for His provision and protection.

SUPPLICATION: *Father, thank You for the light You shine on my life and the taste of Your glory I carry in my heart. Help me to cherish the promise of an eternal future with You and hold on to it no matter what I am facing. Help me to grow in my walk with You, to remain in Your grace, and to keep my complete trust in You tonight. All praise and glory to You. Amen.*

Psalm 85

Even when we go through times or seasons when we stray from God's presence, His truth and righteousness work to restore us to Himself because His love for us is so great. It's comforting to know that He is always ready to forgive and bring us back into His grace. As tonight's psalm says, His unfailing love and the joy of His salvation bring the restoration we need to begin again.

Breathe out the sorrows and regrets from the day, and inhale God's life-giving presence and love. Soak in the strength and renewal His Word of truth gives, and rest in His care. Clear your mind of any distractions by letting go of the anxious thoughts from today and your to-do list for tomorrow, focusing instead on God's faithfulness and love.

You, LORD, showed favor to Your land;
    You restored the fortunes of Jacob.
You forgave the iniquity of Your people
    and covered all their sins.
You set aside all Your wrath
    and turned from Your fierce anger.
Restore us again, God our Savior,
    and put away Your displeasure toward us.
Will You be angry with us forever?
    Will You prolong Your anger through all generations?
Will You not revive us again,
    that Your people may rejoice in You?
Show us Your unfailing love, LORD,
    and grant us Your salvation.
I will listen to what God the LORD says;
    He promises peace to His people, His faithful servants—
    but let them not turn to folly.
Surely His salvation is near those who fear Him,
    that His glory may dwell in our land.
Love and faithfulness meet together;
    righteousness and peace kiss each other.
Faithfulness springs forth from the earth,
    and righteousness looks down from heaven.

The LORD will indeed give what is good,
and our land will yield its harvest.
Righteousness goes before Him
and prepares the way for His steps.

PSALM 85

ADORATION: Meditating on God's love, truth, and righteousness will renew your mind and refresh your spirit, awakening a new longing for the Lord and His ways within you. He will lighten your heart with His forgiveness and love. Praise Him now for His goodness to you.

CONFESSION: Confess any sin the Lord has convicted you of, repenting and asking for His forgiveness. Know His love, poured out for you, covers all your sin and shame.

THANKSGIVING: Rejoice in the righteousness of the Lord, thinking of the ways He has been faithful in your life. Thank Him for the times when He has healed you and restored you. Thank Him for the times when He has blessed you with a plentiful harvest.

SUPPLICATION: *Lord, I'm both humbled and grateful I can come to You without fear, knowing Your forgiveness awaits. Your healing and restoration are what I need tonight and every night. I look to You as my Light to guide me into a safe, quiet place where I can rest. Your faithfulness to me is amazing. All glory to You. Amen.*

Psalm 86

Tonight's psalm reminds us that God is, and always will be, our greatest help when we face trials or tribulations. Trials can be confusing and leave us wondering what, when, and how to move forward. He has the solutions, He knows the perfect path to take, and He is faithful to complete what He's started in our lives. The key to our peace through it all is to remain focused on Him and draw from His strength and direction.

Take a moment to still your mind and offer your struggles up to Him. Allow this unburdening of your heart to usher in the peace and rest you so long for tonight. He wants to bless you with His help. He is ready to provide all that you need.

Listen, LORD, and answer me,
for I am poor and needy.
Protect my life, for I am faithful.
You are my God; save Your servant who trusts in You.
Be gracious to me, Lord,
for I call to You all day long.
Bring joy to Your servant's life,
because I appeal to You, Lord.
For You, Lord, are kind and ready to forgive,
abounding in faithful love to all who call on You.
LORD, hear my prayer;
listen to my cries for mercy.
I call on You in the day of my distress,
for You will answer me. . . .
Teach me Your way, LORD,
and I will live by Your truth.
Give me an undivided mind to fear Your name.
I will praise You with all my heart, Lord my God,
and will honor Your name forever.
For your faithful love for me is great,
and You rescue my life from the depths of Sheol. . . .
Turn to me and be gracious to me.
Give Your strength to Your servant; . . .
Show me a sign of Your goodness;

my enemies will see and be put to shame
because You, LORD, have helped and comforted me.

ADORATION: Take a moment to focus your thoughts on God's sovereignty, His power, love, and might that rule over all the earth. Know He is in complete control of your world and only He can do the wondrous things you desire and need in your life. Think of all His mighty deeds you have witnessed, answered prayers and amazing acts in your life and the lives around you. Rest in the Lord's strength knowing He always has been and always will be Your help.

CONFESSION: Confess any fear and doubts that are keeping you from surrendering to Him, along with any lack of trust that He will be your help even in the toughest situations. Ask for the Lord to show you His mercy and grace, then receive it.

THANKSGIVING: Think of a time when God delivered you from your distress. Thank Him for the ways He has helped you and for the times when He has comforted you. Praise Him for the good things He has done in your life.

SUPPLICATION: *Lord, I call upon You now—for help, for comfort, for provision, and for strength. My eyes are on You and You alone. Teach me Your ways and sustain me through all that doesn't make sense right now. Guide me, protect me, and sustain me through this night. In Jesus' name, I pray. Amen.*

Psalm 87

Tonight's psalm paints a beautiful picture of God's return from heaven to earth when He will rule from His city on a hill—Jerusalem. Believers from every tribe and nation will bow down and worship Him. As we picture this, we are reminded of our bright eternal future with God. While God hasn't returned to earth in power and glory yet, we can all rest—no matter where we are or what goes on around us—we are secure in Him.

He has founded His city on the holy mountain.
The LORD loves the gates of Zion
more than all the other dwellings of Jacob.
Glorious things are said of you,
city of God:
"I will record Rahab and Babylon
among those who acknowledge Me—
Philistia too, and Tyre, along with Cush—
and will say, 'This one was born in Zion.'"
Indeed, of Zion it will be said,
"This one and that one were born in her,
and the Most High Himself will establish her."
The LORD will write in the register of the peoples:
"This one was born in Zion."
As they make music they will sing,
"All my fountains are in you."

PSALM 87

ADORATION: Close your eyes and imagine a brilliant city filled with the glory of God sitting upon a hill, shining its light into the darkness, giving life from its springs to its inhabitants. Hear its inhabitants sing, with one voice, the most beautiful song of praise to God, accompanied by stringed instruments played by musicians strumming a tune as old as time. This is the promise of God's kingdom here on earth. Find rest in the presence of God; dwell in the safety of His city; worship Him for the joy that is ours through Him.

CONFESSION: Bring your struggles to the Lord, confessing any sin that is hindering your relationship with Him. Ask Him to draw you near to Him with His forgiveness and to help you to resist everything that distracts you in your relationship with Him.

THANKSGIVING: Praise the name of the Lord, rejoicing in His promises. Thank Him for the times when He has shown you His mercy and grace. Thank Him for His faithfulness in your life and for the hope of an eternity spent with Him.

SUPPLICATION: *Father, knowing You are Lord over all the nations, all the tribes, all the peoples, and over my life is a gift and a source of peace. I put my trust in You and believe in Your plans for my future. Help me to remember Your majesty when facing difficult times. Help me to rest securely in You tonight and into a new day. May Your grace sustain me and Your mercy bless me in restoring my soul. All praise and glory to You. Amen.*

Psalm 88

In tonight's psalm, the author so eloquently expresses his hardships, wrestling with his own mortality. But the psalmist doesn't stop there: He also directs his pleas to the Lord, looking to Him for help and comfort. God listens to his morning and evening prayers, just as He listens to you when you call upon His name. You are never left alone to struggle; God is always with you.

Take a moment now to release the troubles of your heart to Him. Embrace the truth that God is your strength when you're depleted and your sorrow threatens to overtake you. You can always turn to God to express your deepest fears and worries to Him, knowing He is there every time you call upon Him.

> LORD, You are the God who saves me;
>   day and night I cry out to You.
> May my prayer come before You;
>   turn Your ear to my cry.
> I am overwhelmed with troubles
>   and my life draws near to death.
> I am counted among those who go down to the pit;
>   I am like one without strength. . . .
> You have put me in the lowest pit,
>   in the darkest depths. . . .
> You have taken from me my closest friends
>   and have made me repulsive to them.
> I am confined and cannot escape;
>   my eyes are dim with grief.
> I call to You, LORD, every day;
>   I spread out my hands to You. . . .
> Are Your wonders known in the place of darkness,
>   or Your righteous deeds in the land of oblivion?
> But I cry to You for help, LORD;
>   in the morning my prayer comes before You. . . .
> Your wrath has swept over me;
>   Your terrors have destroyed me.
> All day long they surround me like a flood;

they have completely engulfed me.
You have taken from me friend and neighbor—
darkness is my closest friend.

PSALM 88:1-4, 6, 8-9, 12-13, 16-18

ADORATION: When we pray to God, we may not always find relief right away, but God's Word makes it clear that He is always with us, and He listens when we call upon Him. We don't have to be cheerful to come to the Lord; we can come to Him with any and all emotions and find rest. Praise Him for the care He shows by hearing and receiving our prayers.

CONFESSION: Sometimes, when life is hard and we are facing seemingly impossible circumstances, we begin to doubt God's goodness and faithfulness. Confess any fears and doubts you have. Lift them to God and ask Him to restore your faith in Him.

THANKSGIVING: Think of the ways God has kept His promises in your life. Thank Him for His faithfulness and for the times when He has helped you and delivered you. Thank Him for comforting you tonight.

SUPPLICATION: *Father, I pour out my heart to You tonight without holding back. Sustain me through my circumstances that deplete my strength. Forgive me for doubting You when times are hard. Restore my faith in Your power and presence and help me to truly rest in You as I end this day. Help me to keep my thoughts fixed on You. In Jesus' name, I pray. Amen.*

Psalm 89

The Bible reminds us over and over again of God's loving-kindness and of His promise to preserve us and protect us, to set us apart for His glory. He knows the hearts of those who love Him, and He sees when they are afflicted. He will strengthen us through the day, and His hand will sustain us through the night. We are exalted by His righteousness; nothing can change His love for His people.

Tonight, let us turn away from anything or anyone who diminishes our belief in the all-powerful God; let us place our trust in His mighty presence in our lives.

> I will sing about the LORD's faithful love forever;
> I will proclaim Your faithfulness to all generations
> with my mouth.
> For I will declare,
> "Faithful love is built up forever;
> You establish Your faithfulness in the heavens."
> The LORD said,
> "I have made a covenant with My chosen one;
> I have sworn an oath to David My servant:
> 'I will establish your offspring forever
> and build up your throne for all generations.'" Selah . . .
> LORD God of Armies,
> who is strong like You, LORD?
> Your faithfulness surrounds You. . . .
> The heavens are Yours; the earth also is Yours.
> The world and everything in it—You founded them. . . .
> You have a mighty arm;
> Your hand is powerful;
> Your right hand is lifted high.
> Righteousness and justice are the foundation
> of Your throne; . . .
> You once spoke in a vision to Your faithful ones
> and said, "I have granted help to a warrior;
> I have exalted one chosen from the people.
> I have found David My servant;
> I have anointed him with My sacred oil. . . .

My faithfulness and love will be with him,
and through My name
his horn will be exalted. . . .
But You have spurned and rejected him;
You have become enraged with Your anointed. . . .
All who pass by plunder him;
he has become an object of ridicule
to his neighbors. . . .
How long, LORD? Will You hide forever?
Will Your anger keep burning like fire?
Remember how short my life is. . . .
Blessed be the LORD forever.
Amen and amen.

PSALM 89:1–4, 8, 11, 13–14, 19–20, 24, 38, 41, 46–47, 52 CSB

ADORATION: The psalmist reminds us of God's power, sovereignty, and faithfulness in this passage. He reminds us that we can completely put our trust in Him because He is our Rock and Savior, our Father and Redeemer. Allow His constant presence to lighten your heart as you prepare for sleep tonight.

CONFESSION: Confess any times you relied on your own strength instead of asking the Lord for His help and guidance. Turn to Him and ask for His forgiveness, knowing that He listens and forgives freely.

THANKSGIVING: Rejoice in the faithfulness of the Lord, for His power and might that are with you always. Thank Him for the blessings and favor He has poured upon you.

SUPPLICATION: *Lord, You are a God who doesn't change, and I am grateful. Even when I don't understand some circumstances in life, I know You are with me and keeping Your promises to me. Thank You for Your faithfulness in the past as well as in my future. Sustain me this night for a deep, peaceful sleep, and fill me with Your strength as I go into a new day tomorrow. All glory to You. Amen.*

Psalm 90

In our ever-changing world, we can find comfort in the everlasting and unchanging nature of God, knowing He has always existed, and He always will. He is the Alpha and the Omega—the One who gave us life, who will guide and lead us through our time here on earth, and the One who will take us to His eternal dwelling to rest.

To begin tonight's reading, take time to be still and breathe out the stresses of the day. Clear your mind as you receive the following words from our Lord. Allow His truth to focus your heart on eternity and give you a new perspective tonight.

Lord, You have been our dwelling place
*   throughout all generations.*
Before the mountains were born
*   or You brought forth the whole world,*
*   from everlasting to everlasting You are God....*
A thousand years in Your sight
*   are like a day that has just gone by,*
*   or like a watch in the night....*
In the morning it springs up new,
*   but by evening it is dry and withered....*
You have set our iniquities before You,
*   our secret sins in the light of Your presence....*
Our days may come to seventy years,
*   or eighty, if our strength endures;*
yet the best of them are but trouble and sorrow,
*   for they quickly pass, and we fly away....*
Teach us to number our days,
*   that we may gain a heart of wisdom....*
Satisfy us in the morning with Your unfailing love,
*   that we may sing for joy and be glad all our days.*
Make us glad for as many days as You have afflicted us,
*   for as many years as we have seen trouble.*
May Your deeds be shown to Your servants,
*   Your splendor to their children.*
May the favor of the Lord our God rest on us;

establish the work of our hands for us—
yes, establish the work of our hands.

PSALM 90:1-2, 4, 6, 8, 10, 12, 14-17

ADORATION: God's Word reminds us He is everlasting—He was, He is, and He is yet to come, meaning He is our past, present, and future. He is our constant in this changing world. Let us acknowledge and exalt Him for this amazing fact. We can dwell in His safety for all the days of our lives, and we can rest securely in His hands every night.

CONFESSION: We can never hide our sins from God. Our secret sins, the darkness within us, is always brought to light in His presence. So, tonight, let's not hold on to our sins and struggles, but let's release them to God now. Confession is not to inform God of our sins but to come to God with our sins to be redeemed and restored by His grace and love.

THANKSGIVING: Rejoice in His unfailing love and compassion. Thank the Lord for fully knowing you and fully loving you. Thank Him that He is unchanging and steady.

SUPPLICATION: *Father, I confess that sometimes I take my life for granted. Help me to number my days and live as though every single day matters. Point my thoughts and motives toward You, and bless the work of my hands, no matter how small or insignificant a job it might be. Bless me with Your peace and serenity tonight as I entrust my life, body, and spirit to You. In Jesus' name. Amen.*

Psalm 91

Hardship is an inevitability in this life, but we have a God who is with us through every season and struggle we encounter. When we need protection to keep us from harm, whether mentally, physically, or spiritually, God is here for us. He is our Safe Refuge and Protective Shield, our Strong Fortress and Deliverer.

Tonight, open your heart to God's presence. He is for you; He will not abandon you. Ask Him to speak to you now through His Word and allow yourself to be comforted by His presence.

> Whoever dwells in the shelter of the Most High
>   will rest in the shadow of the Almighty.
> I will say of the LORD, "He is my refuge and my fortress,
>   my God, in whom I trust."
> Surely He will save you
>   from the fowler's snare
>   and from the deadly pestilence.
> He will cover you with His feathers,
>   and under His wings you will find refuge;
>   His faithfulness will be your shield and rampart.
> You will not fear the terror of night,
>   nor the arrow that flies by day,
> nor the pestilence that stalks in the darkness,
>   nor the plague that destroys at midday. . . .
> If you say, "The LORD is my refuge,"
>   and you make the Most High your dwelling,
> no harm will overtake you,
>   no disaster will come near your tent.
> For He will command His angels concerning you
>   to guard you in all your ways;
> they will lift you up in their hands,
>   so that you will not strike your foot against a stone. . . .
> "Because he loves me," says the LORD, "I will rescue him;
>   I will protect him, for he acknowledges My name.
> He will call on Me, and I will answer him;
>   I will be with him in trouble,

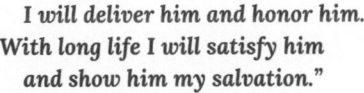

I will deliver him and honor him.
With long life I will satisfy him
and show him my salvation."

PSALM 91:1-6, 9-12, 14-16

ADORATION: As you lie down to sleep, be filled with the presence of the Almighty, and take refuge from the worries of the day in His calming and reassuring arms. When you do, remember that you are safe and secure there; no one and nothing can overcome you. Give Him praise for His great love for you.

CONFESSION: Think of a time when your fears were greater than your faith in God. Confess any fears and doubts you are still struggling with now. Allow His voice to remind you of His power, provision, and protection. Ask Him to increase your faith in the face of fear.

THANKSGIVING: Rejoice in God and the way He watches over you. Praise Him for His faithfulness. Thank Him for the times when He has protected you and for the times when He has helped you and delivered you.

SUPPLICATION: *Father, I want to think only of You and how great and almighty You are. Cover me and keep me safe and secure this night as I trust in You. Deliver me from my fears and worries; hold me and sustain me tonight and help me to face tomorrow in Your strength. All glory be to You. Amen.*

Psalm 92

The Bible tells us that cultivating a heart of worship will bring a fresh perspective to our lives and help us stand firmly in the Lord. As you wind down from the day, let your heart relax and remain open to Him. Clear your mind and reflect on the beauty He's put into your life, the blessings He's given you. Ask God to refresh you tonight with His truth from the psalms and to remind you of His faithfulness. Allow His voice to lead you to a quiet place where you can rest.

As you praise God, let His joy and peace lighten your heart and calm your mind as you prepare for rest.

It is good to give thanks to the LORD,
    to sing praises to the Most High.
It is good to proclaim Your unfailing love in the morning,
    Your faithfulness in the evening,
accompanied by a ten-stringed instrument, a harp,
    and the melody of a lyre.
You thrill me, LORD, with all You have done for me!
    I sing for joy because of what You have done.
O LORD, what great works You do!
    And how deep are Your thoughts.
Only a simpleton would not know,
    and only a fool would not understand this:
Though the wicked sprout like weeds
    and evildoers flourish,
    they will be destroyed forever.
But You, O LORD, will be exalted forever.
Your enemies, LORD, will surely perish;
    all evildoers will be scattered.
But You have made me as strong as a wild ox.
    You have anointed me with the finest oil.
My eyes have seen the downfall of my enemies;
    my ears have heard the defeat of my wicked opponents.
But the godly will flourish like palm trees
    and grow strong like the cedars of Lebanon.

For they are transplanted to the LORD's own house.
They flourish in the courts of our God.
Even in old age they will still produce fruit;
they will remain vital and green.
They will declare, "The LORD is just!
He is my rock!
There is no evil in Him!"

PSALM 92 NLT

ADORATION: Take a few moments to meditate on the faithfulness of the Lord, as described in this psalm. Lift your burdens to Him and allow His glory and peace to fill your heart and mind. Reflect on the promises of His faithfulness in your life. Take a moment to praise Him for His goodness to you.

CONFESSION: Are your prayers filled with more asking than thanksgiving? If so, confess when you have neglected praising Him. Ask Him to fill your heart with gratitude and your mind with positive thoughts.

THANKSGIVING: Praise the Lord for His steadfast love and care for you, He is faithful. Thank Him for the wonderful things He has done in your life. Thank Him for being the One on whom you can depend.

SUPPLICATION: *Lord, words don't adequately describe the praise and thanksgiving I have for You. You have saved me, protected me, and provided for me. You have blessed me, filled me with joy, and loved me unconditionally. Because of You I have purpose in my life. Because of You, I have eternal life with You. I am forever grateful. In Jesus' precious name, I pray. Amen.*

Psalm 93

Tonight's psalm reminds us that the Lord is stronger than any storm we face. His power and strength can sustain us during the longest drought; He will keep us anchored no matter how wild the waves of life are. We can know, without a doubt, that He is always in control, and He uses His power for our good.

As you wind down from the day, ask the Lord to speak to you with clarity and assurance. Allow the power of His truth to comfort you through this night for a sweet and peaceful sleep.

> The LORD reigns, He is robed in majesty;
>> the LORD is robed in majesty and armed with strength;
>> indeed, the world is established, firm and secure.
> Your throne was established long ago;
>> You are from all eternity.
> The seas have lifted up, LORD,
>> the seas have lifted up their voice;
>> the seas have lifted up their pounding waves.
> Mightier than the thunder of the great waters,
>> mightier than the breakers of the sea—
>> the LORD on high is mighty.
> Your statutes, LORD, stand firm;
>> holiness adorns Your house
>> for endless days.
>
> **PSALM 93**

ADORATION: Close your eyes and visualize the Lord as your King, clothed with majesty, reigning over all the earth, reigning over your life. Know, in His power and strength, He can strike down the storms that threaten to overtake you. Picture the waves of the seas rising against you. Listen to the pounding of the waves as they crash back and forth. Feel the Lord's mighty hands strike down the waters; hear His thundering voice over the roar of the mighty seas. The same power that established the world and created the seas is the power that establishes your steps, keeping you safe and secure. Praise Almighty God for how great He is!

CONFESSION: Think of a time when you buckled under the pressure of life and abandoned the ways of the Lord; ask for His forgiveness. Ask Him to make your steps firm and secure, just like He did with the foundation of the world.

THANKSGIVING: Rejoice in the power and strength of the Lord. Thank Him for the times when He has protected you from the storm. Thank Him for the times when He delivered you with His mighty hands.

SUPPLICATION: *Lord God, my heart is moved at how very great and mighty You are. Who am I that You, the Creator of the universe, loves me, saved me, and will carry me through this night? Help me to follow Your commands and keep me in Your perfect peace no matter what I am facing. Protect me as I close this day and rest safely in Your arms. I love You, Lord, and I want to love You more. Amen.*

Psalm 94

Tonight's psalm reminds us that God will sustain His people until the day He casts judgment on the wicked. He is the righteous Judge who will right all the wrongs in the end to restore His world and rescue His people. We can find incredible comfort and peace when we put our trust in the Lord and allow Him to administer His mercy and justice in our lives.

Lift your hurts and pain to the Lord now and open your heart to hear His Word. Ask Him to instill in you the power of His ways so there is no doubt that you can rest safe and secure in Him.

The LORD is a God who avenges.
O God who avenges, shine forth.
Rise up, Judge of the earth;
pay back to the proud what they deserve....
They say, "The LORD does not see;
the God of Jacob takes no notice."
Take notice, you senseless ones among the people;
you fools, when will you become wise?
Does He who fashioned the ear not hear?
Does He who formed the eye not see?
Does He who disciplines nations not punish?
Does He who teaches mankind lack knowledge?
The LORD knows all human plans;
He knows that they are futile....
For the LORD will not reject His people;
He will never forsake His inheritance.
Judgment will again be founded on righteousness,
and all the upright in heart will follow it....
When I said, "My foot is slipping,"
Your unfailing love, LORD, supported me.
When anxiety was great within me,
Your consolation brought me joy....
The wicked band together against the righteous
and condemn the innocent to death.

But the LORD has become my fortress,
and my God the rock in whom I take refuge.
He will repay them for their sins
and destroy them for their wickedness;
the LORD our God will destroy them.

PSALM 94:1-2, 7-11, 14-15, 18-19, 21-23

ADORATION: The corruption of this world is temporary. We know this is true because our God, who formed our ears, can hear the boasts of the wicked. Our God, who formed our eyes, can see the injustices being committed. And until the day He returns to cast judgment on the world, God will sustain us with His mighty hands, strengthening us in the day, comforting us in the night.

CONFESSION: Think of a time when someone hurt you and you retaliated rather than waiting on the Lord. Confess any anger or bitterness in your heart. Ask God for His forgiveness and for His help with forgiving the person who hurt you.

THANKSGIVING: Rejoice in the Lord and think about the good things He has blessed you with. Praise Him for His mercy and justice. Thank Him for sustaining you with His unfailing love.

SUPPLICATION: *Father, it's hard to see injustice in my life and in others' lives around me and sit idly by. So I pray to You now—for faith to believe that You truly see and that You will deal with those who commit wrong, all in Your time and in Your way. Help me to remain focused on You and Your Word so I can remain strong and not get discouraged or lose faith. You are a great and mighty God, and I'm so glad You're in control. All praise to You. Amen.*

Psalm 95

Tonight's psalm is a beautiful reminder of the greatness of our God. He has shown His love since the beginning of time. We want so much for Him to love and bless us with His presence and provision—He wants so much for us to devote our hearts to Him. When we listen to His voice and follow His ways, we will find the peace and rest we need and desire from Him.

As you read and meditate on His Word, ask the Lord to speak to your heart and draw you closer to Him, the God who holds the universe in His hands. There is no safer place than to be in His arms.

Come, let us sing for joy to the LORD;
　　let us shout aloud to the Rock of our salvation.
Let us come before Him with thanksgiving
　　and extol Him with music and song.
For the LORD is the great God,
　　the great King above all gods.
In His hand are the depths of the earth,
　　and the mountain peaks belong to Him.
The sea is His, for He made it,
　　and His hands formed the dry land.
Come, let us bow down in worship,
　　let us kneel before the LORD our Maker;
for He is our God
　　and we are the people of His pasture,
　　the flock under His care.
Today, if only you would hear His voice,
"Do not harden your hearts as you did at Meribah,
　　as you did that day at Massah in the wilderness,
where your ancestors tested Me;
　　they tried Me, though they had seen what I did.
For forty years I was angry with that generation;
　　I said, 'They are a people whose hearts go astray,
　　and they have not known My ways.'

So I declared on oath in My anger,
'They shall never enter My rest.'"

PSALM 95

ADORATION: Tonight, reflect on who God is to you. He is the Rock you can count on, the Creator who delights in you and sustains you, and the King who cares for you and protects you. Worship the Lord for who He is.

CONFESSION: Think of a time when you hardened your heart to the Lord and followed a path that led you astray. Acknowledge any unconfessed sin from that time. Ask God to forgive you for your mistakes and help you move forward on His path of life and righteousness.

THANKSGIVING: Worship the Lord in your heart, thanking Him for securing your future as you trust in Him. Thank Him for the ways in which He provides for you and protects you.

SUPPLICATION: *Father, my heart swells when I think of all You have done, not only for humanity and creation, but for me and my life. Help me to cling to Your goodness when my heart is heavy and to trust in You no matter my circumstances. I want to hear Your voice and go where You lead. I know only You can provide space where my soul can be at rest. I love You and fix my thoughts on You now. Amen.*

Psalm 96

There are an endless number of inspiring people, places, and things that capture our focus and garner our attention. Yet God, in all His glory, wants us to fix our eyes on and be enraptured with Him first and foremost—the Creator of everything else. The same hands that created the heavens and the earth are the hands that want to lift your burdens and give you rest. No one else can do this like God does.

Tonight, as you read God's Word and reflect on His creation, let your heart be filled with the fullness of His grace in your life. He loves you and longs to be praised by you.

Sing to the LORD a new song;
   sing to the LORD, all the earth.
Sing to the LORD, praise His name;
   proclaim His salvation day after day.
Declare His glory among the nations,
   His marvelous deeds among all peoples.
For great is the LORD and most worthy of praise;
   He is to be feared above all gods.
For all the gods of the nations are idols,
   but the LORD made the heavens. . . .
Ascribe to the LORD, all you families of nations,
   ascribe to the LORD glory and strength.
Ascribe to the LORD the glory due His name;
   bring an offering and come into His courts.
Worship the LORD in the splendor of His holiness;
   tremble before Him, all the earth.
Say among the nations, "The LORD reigns."
   The world is firmly established, it cannot be moved;
   He will judge the peoples with equity.
Let the heavens rejoice, let the earth be glad;
   let the sea resound, and all that is in it. . . .
Let all creation rejoice before the LORD, for He comes,
   He comes to judge the earth.
He will judge the world in righteousness
   and the peoples in His faithfulness.

PSALM 96:1–5, 7–11, 13

ADORATION: The psalmist reminds us that God's beautiful creation is filled with His glory, revealing He is the one, true God. Find comfort in knowing you serve the Lord over all the nations, the Creator of the heavens and the earth. Worship Him and praise His name for all that He has done.

CONFESSION: Think of a time when you had the opportunity to tell someone about the glory of God, but fear prevented you from sharing the Good News. Ask God for His forgiveness and for His strength and courage the next time an opportunity arises to declare His marvelous deeds.

THANKSGIVING: Praise the Lord for His glory and strength. Thank Him for setting you apart for the glory of His name. Thank Him for the beautiful blessings He has given you and for the wonderful things He has done for you.

SUPPLICATION: *Lord, I want to give You the glory due Your name and worship You with my whole heart. Because of You, my life is rich in love and filled with purpose. Because of You, I can be at rest and have supernatural peace. Help me to claim these promises today and to share in Your glory with others and give You all the credit You deserve. Let my love for You be contagious in a way that leads others to You. In Jesus' great name, I pray. Amen.*

Psalm 97

Tonight, allow yourself to relax and experience a deep peace that comes from God. Breathe in His power and love; breathe out your fears and worries. Lift your weaknesses to Him and open your eyes to the presence of the Lord around and within your being.

As you read this wonderful song of praise, take delight in His glory and lift your spirit to rejoice in His name. Know that the Lord reigns over all the earth as well as your life. There isn't anything you are facing that He isn't aware of. If you cast your burdens to Him, He will receive them and reassure you in His loving care. Feel His joy warm your heart and refresh your soul as no one or nothing else can.

The LORD reigns, let the earth be glad;
let the distant shores rejoice.
Clouds and thick darkness surround Him;
righteousness and justice are the foundation of His throne.
Fire goes before Him
and consumes His foes on every side.
His lightning lights up the world;
the earth sees and trembles.
The mountains melt like wax before the LORD,
before the Lord of all the earth.
The heavens proclaim His righteousness,
and all peoples see His glory.
All who worship images are put to shame,
those who boast in idols—
worship Him, all you gods! . . .
For You, LORD, are the Most High over all the earth;
You are exalted far above all gods.
Let those who love the LORD hate evil,
for He guards the lives of His faithful ones
and delivers them from the hand of the wicked.
Light shines on the righteous
and joy on the upright in heart.

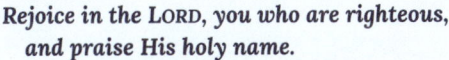

Rejoice in the LORD, you who are righteous,
and praise His holy name.

PSALM 97:1–7, 9–12

ADORATION: The Bible tells us that nature reveals the glory and the power of its Creator. The lightning flashes His brilliance and strength; the mountains display His majesty and power; the fire demonstrates His sovereignty as it consumes His enemies by day and guides His people by night. Know that the same power that sends bolts of lightning across the sky, that forms and moves mountains, and that sets the fire ablaze is the power protecting you and preserving you tonight.

CONFESSION: Think of something in your life you prioritize over God. It could be a person such as a spouse or a child; it could be a job or a hobby. Confess this wrongful prioritization to God and ask for His forgiveness. Ask for Him to help you prioritize spending time with Him above all else.

THANKSGIVING: Rejoice in the Lord. Thank Him for revealing His glory to you and shining His light upon you in the darkness of the night. Thank Him for the times when He has protected you. Thank Him for the times when He has delivered you.

SUPPLICATION: *Father, I cast my cares on You tonight. Help any unbelief that lingers as I navigate living in a fallen world. Help me to remember that You reign, that You will protect me, that You will sustain me as I seek Your face and Your will for my life. May Your light guide my steps and keep me from temptation. Let Your favor rest on me tonight and into tomorrow as I dwell in Your peace. In Jesus' name. Amen.*

Psalm 98

As you prepare to receive God's Word tonight, clear your mind of any distractions. Ask God to help you focus on Him, not on any worries that linger in your mind. Allow the Word to renew your spirit.

The Bible reminds us we do not have to be afraid of the evil in this world because our victory is in the Lord; He has already won the battles we face. And one of the best ways to remind us of the Lord's victory is through praise—especially when we don't feel like expressing it. Praise turns our focus from the darkness that worry and anxiety bring and fixes our gaze on the goodness of our Father.

Tonight, let's open our hearts to the Lord and praise Him for who He is and how He's working in our lives.

> Sing a new song to the LORD,
> for He has performed wonders;
> His right hand and holy arm
> have won Him victory.
> The LORD has made His victory known;
> He has revealed His righteousness
> in the sight of the nations.
> He has remembered His love
> and faithfulness to the house of Israel;
> all the ends of the earth
> have seen our God's victory.
> Let the whole earth shout to the LORD;
> be jubilant, shout for joy, and sing.
> Sing to the LORD with the lyre,
> with the lyre and melodious song.
> With trumpets and the blast of the ram's horn
> shout triumphantly
> in the presence of the LORD, our King.
> Let the sea and all that fills it,
> the world and those who live in it, resound.
> Let the rivers clap their hands;
> let the mountains shout together for joy

before the LORD,
for He is coming to judge the earth.
He will judge the world righteously
and the peoples fairly.

PSALM 98 CSB

ADORATION: When we are overwhelmed, this psalm reminds us of the joy and victory we have in the Lord, calming our minds and soothing our souls. Know His love and faithfulness will sustain you through life's ups and downs. Know you can rest safely in His arms tonight.

CONFESSION: Think of a time when you cast unnecessary judgment on someone, confessing any arrogance in your heart. Ask for God's forgiveness. Ask for Him to remind you that He is the righteous Judge who will bring the best type of mercy and justice to our world.

THANKSGIVING: Think of all the marvelous things God has done in your life, from small to large. Thank Him for the blessings He has given you in the past. Thank Him for His love and faithfulness that sustain you in your present.

SUPPLICATION: *Lord, I am so blessed to call You Father. I'm so blessed to call You friend. I open my heart and life to You now; I want Your wisdom and goodness to guide me. Increase my faith. Please keep me in perfect peace tonight as I surrender my cares of this day to You and find rest in You. Lord, You are the One from whom all blessings flow. Amen.*

Psalm 99

God loves justice; He loves fairness. And He comes through in our lives by executing His justice in the same way today as He did when Moses, Aaron, and Samuel called on His name. Take time now to quiet your mind by focusing on the goodness of God and the goodness of His loving justice. Focus on His righteous and mighty acts throughout history and in your life today. He is *the* righteous Judge you can trust to always do what is best for you.

As you read tonight's psalm, listen for His voice to speak to your heart. Allow His Truth to fill your heart with joy and peace as you prepare for rest.

> The Lord reigns,
>   let the nations tremble;
> He sits enthroned between the cherubim,
>   let the earth shake.
> Great is the Lord in Zion;
>   He is exalted over all the nations.
> Let them praise your great and awesome name—
>   He is holy.
> The King is mighty, He loves justice—
>   You have established equity;
> in Jacob You have done
>   what is just and right.
> Exalt the Lord our God
>   and worship at His footstool;
>   He is holy.
> Moses and Aaron were among His priests,
>   Samuel was among those who called on His name;
> they called on the Lord
>   and He answered them.
> He spoke to them from the pillar of cloud;
>   they kept His statutes and the decrees He gave them.
> Lord our God,
>   You answered them;
> You were to Israel a forgiving God,

> *though You punished their misdeeds.*
> *Exalt the LORD our God*
> *and worship at His holy mountain,*
> *for the LORD our God is holy.*

PSALM 99

ADORATION: Meditate on the holiness of the Lord, as outlined in today's psalm. His goodness resounds throughout the heavens and the earth. Feel the nations tremble and the earth shake at the sound of His name. Rejoice in His great and awesome name. Feel Him renew your spirit and comfort your soul. Lift your spirit to exalt the Almighty King who rules over the nations with His power and might. Be comforted by His powerful presence tonight.

CONFESSION: Confess the times when your words and actions did not reflect your love for God or His holiness. Ask Him to help you say and do what is right in His eyes.

THANKSGIVING: Rejoice in the holiness of the Lord, praising Him for His justice and mercy. Thank Him for the times He has forgiven you and given you grace. Thank Him for the prayers He has answered in your life.

SUPPLICATION: *Father, I call upon You tonight, and I wait expectantly to hear from You. Please give me patience and faith when I find myself in unfair situations. I trust that You will intervene and bring justice as You also show mercy to everyone involved. I ask that You will lead me to a safe, secure place where I am able to rest tonight in Your care. I love You and thank You for the peace that only You can give. In Jesus' name. Amen.*

Psalm 100

Tonight's psalm invites us to joyfully enter the presence of God and find rest in His truth that transcends time. But how do we do that when we're burdened by the challenges we're facing? As much as it goes against our natural inclination, praise and worship, for even the smallest of things, transforms and lifts our hearts out of despair into the heights of our gracious Lord.

Take a moment to breathe out the day and inhale God's pure and holy presence. Allow your heart and mind to be still and soak in God's faithfulness and love for you. Know He is the Lord your God and invite His spirit into your thoughts. Open your heart to Him and allow His truth to comfort you, bringing you His joy and peace.

> Shout for joy to the LORD, all the earth.
> Worship the LORD with gladness;
>   come before Him with joyful songs.
> Know that the LORD is God.
>   It is He who made us, and we are His;
>   we are His people, the sheep of His pasture.
> Enter His gates with thanksgiving
>   and His courts with praise;
>   give thanks to Him and praise His name.
> For the LORD is good and His love endures forever;
>   His faithfulness continues through all generations.

PSALM 100

ADORATION: Meditating on who God is can fill our hearts with joy and peace and comfort us as we prepare for sleep. His Word reminds us that the Lord of all the earth is our creator. Rejoice in the fact that the Lord of all creation is the One who promises to care for you and comfort you every day and every night. Rejoice in the satisfaction that comes only from the Lord. Find peace in His presence.

CONFESSION: Think of the ways you have doubted the faithfulness of God and the truth of His Word, lifting any doubts you have of God's goodness and the truth of His Word to Him tonight. Ask for Him to help your unbelief and help you find your faith once again.

THANKSGIVING: Come before the Lord with thanksgiving and praise. Thank Him for His provision today. Thank Him for His protection tonight. Thank Him for His love that sustains you and His faithfulness that restores you all the days of your life.

SUPPLICATION: *Father, I take great comfort in knowing You are my Shepherd and that You care about every detail of my life. Help my thoughts to be filled with gratitude for all that You do—let me never take Your goodness for granted. I lift up my cares to You and trust that You will be faithful to me now as You have been in my past. Help me to rest securely in knowing that You will provide for my needs—I will not be left wanting. Cover me now and through this night.*

ABOUT PRAY.COM

Pray.com serves millions of Christians worldwide by helping people make prayer a priority in their life. Pray.com is driven by a mission to grow faith, cultivate community, and leave a legacy of helping others.

Pray.com helps people hear the Bible come to life with world-class, faith-based audio content, make prayer a priority with inspiring daily devotions, and experience peace before they go to sleep with *Bedtime Bible Stories* narrated by celebrity voices.

Learn more about Pray.com and access their unique content geared toward sleep by scanning the QR code below!